BEING, LEARNING AND DOING

BEING, LEARNING AND DOING

How Leaders Create Capabilities

Taneisha Ingleton, PhD

BEING, LEARNING AND DOING. Copyright © 2019. Taneisha Ingleton, PhD. All Rights Reserved.

Printed in the United States of America.

No portion of this book may be reproduced, stored in a retrieval system, or transmitted in any form or by any means, except for brief quotations in printed reviews, without the prior written permission of Taneisha Ingleton, PhD.

Unless otherwise indicated, all Scripture quotations are taken from the King James Version.

Book Cover Design by Collin Hugh Bailey.

ISBN: 978-1-949343-53-3 (paperback)

I dedicate this book to all leaders who were told they could not lead.

I also dedicate this book to my daughter, Chrysali. I know that someday on your leadership journey you are going to need this.

ACKNOWLEDGMENTS

To Carmichael Ingleton, my dear husband: thank you for allowing me to fly and for reminding me of my worth.

Thanks to Philando Neil for encouraging me to step out of the familiar and step into the destiny that my heart kept longing for.

Thanks to Toni-Ann Rankine for tricking me into thinking I could meet my own ridiculous deadlines. Your belief in me forced me to do it.

To my team from the National College for Educational Leadership: thank you for allowing me to learn to be more, learn more and do more while leading you.

TABLE OF CONTENTS

Acknowledgments ix
A Note from the Author 1
Understanding the Dimensions 5

Dimension 1 - Leadership As Being 11
    Insight 1: There Is Always A Beginning..................... 11
    Insight 2: The Way You See People Is The Way
    You Lead Them 17
    Insight 3: Your Colleagues Are Not Your
    Competition But Your Reinforcement 22
    Insight 4: You Are More Than Likely Getting
    What You Give 27
    Insight 5: We Grow Talent By Delegating,
    Not Dumping 31
    Insight 6: Power Is Not Leadership 35
    Insight 7: Nothing Needs To Be In It For You 41
    Insight 8: It Requires Strength To Be
    Compassionate... 44
    Insight 9: Praise Elevates.. 49
Reflecting On *The Being* Dimension............................... 52

Dimension 2: Leadership As Learning.............................. 55

    Insight 10: Learning Through Being Slighted 56

    Insight 11: Learning To Leverage Your Youth............. 61

    Insight 12: There Is Beauty In Ignoring:
Learn To Master It 68

    Insight 13: Being Present With Your Ears Can Be
More Valuable Than Being Present With Your Voice .. 70

    Insight 14: Learn Through Opportunities 75

    Insight 15: Learn To Give And Receive Feedback 77

    Insight 16: Learning By Following Others................ 80

Reflecting On *The Learning* Dimension 85

Dimension 3: Leadership As Doing 89

    Insight 17: "Doing" Through Presence 92

    Insight 18: "Doing" Through Structures.................... 94

    Insight 19: "Doing" Through Visioning..................... 95

    Insight 20: "Doing" Through Core Values 100

I Am Committed To *"Doing"* 105

About the Author 113

END NOTES 115

That still small voice that said, "follow your dreams" must have been the Christ.

A NOTE FROM THE AUTHOR

I often do many presentations and then moved into writing leadership blogs. I switched to social media full force and started to write motivational pieces on leadership, all triggered from my own convictions and experiences. My social media family and other close friends would send me messages asking when I will be writing a book. They thought the expressions were worth expansion. However, I did not pay them much attention as having written two theses, a dissertation and multiple essays and articles in my academic journey, I was ready and content to write only letters, emails, memos, concept papers and development programmes.

In my early thirties, I joined a group where I interacted with many young people who had such moving perspectives from the leadership they experienced that they lost all forms of expression in their workspaces. Having read so many leadership books, I thought, *'Where is the book that shows how leaders create capabilities?'* Certainly, there is so much that tell you how to be a better person and to fully maximize your potential, but where is the one that offers the naked truth about the things you do that affect your employees and implores you to stop, reflect and change? It was then that I purposed to fit the pieces together that were scattered across so many platforms.

My heart on leadership is simple; it is leading in such a way that you build others to lead as well as, or much better than, you could ever imagine to lead. It is being that individual others will adjust their ways of thinking to emulate, not because it will illuminate them, rather it will create a better space for others. What is there to life really, if our behaviours do not positively impact others? For what do we live, if only power motivates us?

This book was written from a conviction that it is only when we deliberately and purposefully create avenues for others to do better that we truly lead. Strategic priorities, visioneering and critical thinking are big ticket pieces, but they mean little if the result is not building others.

This book is intended to show you how to make the space, time, and thinking to build up a generation that will do better than us. It was the admonition and the vision of

Christ when He said to His disciples: *"Verily, verily, I say unto you, He that believeth on me, the works that I do shall he do also; and greater works than these shall he do." (John 14:12).* Leadership is, at best, a failure, if it does not uplift another in thoughts and explicit and discernible expressions of character and behaviour.

Taneisha Ingleton

UNDERSTANDING THE DIMENSIONS

*The eye sees only what the mind
is prepared to comprehend.*

~ Henri Bergson

I love leadership and I can certainly understand why some would not. We are all different people with singular situations. No one has the same journey to any given destination. Our paths are unique, and our goals are often not connected or complimentary and, in some cases, not even conscious. What is universal and unquestionable is that we all have a place in this life and our behaviours inadvertently affect others, consciously or otherwise. It then behoves us to find a frame to understand our behaviours, and those of others, as our own perspectives are limiting, and we struggle with our own psychological biases. Only when we recognize our failings can we begin to make meaningful change. Only when we begin to perceive our own weaknesses and strengths can we leverage them for victory, not only for our cause but also for others.

If we had all the answers, so many of us would not disagree about so many things. Still, if we all agreed, there would be no diversity and the world would be less than exciting to live in. No wonder the literature on leadership is vast and ever emerging. I have read more than ten thousand references on this very fascinating behaviour. My personal investment each month is a new book on leadership or a reading on leadership development and behaviours. In any given year, I cover more than fifty leadership material by reading alone. I have lost count of the teachings, the mentoring and coaching I do both formally and otherwise. Even with all these interactions and insights, I continue to be in awe of this concept and do spend most waking moments examining it. I examine leadership through Scripture, research, my own observations and practices and still those of the many around me who I have had the privilege to lead.

In my dissertation completed in 2014, I articulated some concepts that ring true everyday and I have co-opted some of them as *insights* in this book. I said then that leadership is an evolutionary phenomenon as the construct shifts with the dawn of almost every decade. It has moved in stages from being hierarchical, power-based, and productivity-driven to appropriating features of transformation, service, collaboration, relationships, ethics, and even love. The leadership journey is so singular and personal, yet so complicated and communal that no one framework or perspective can serve its explanation any justice. More is needed to better understand and implement the lessons this exhilarating process brings. I often question why we make so many mistakes, why we hurt so many people in our spaces, why individuals speak so negatively about their bosses and why some bosses fail to comprehend their employees' needs. How can we be speaking so confidently and requiring others to do the very things we do not and to act on principles with which we are evidently struggling? Seriously, how do we not see our own shortcomings, yet demand high performance from others? How can we do and become better? How can we advance systems, develop processes and spur others to growth? How can we develop organizations that are venerable with strong leaders of conviction and purpose? My desire to respond to these questions have become my life's work.

The book you are reading provides an integrated system of three dimensions of leadership and leadership development that should not be viewed singularly. The same way we live in a world defined by three spatial dimensions of length, width and height, it is the same way complex processes that are inextricably connected mark our development.

Being, Learning and ***Doing*** is a co-active process of leadership and leadership development where lack of growth in one dimension or another does create barriers and roadblocks to a successful leadership journey. The interplay among the three dimensions act as a force of elevated performance connecting in unison who we are with what we experience in this world, and then how we choose to react. Each dimension carries insights and transformative practices informed by years of observations, experiences and decades of research. This book is but one way we can frame leadership and organizational life. It creates a road map, a pathway for understanding, refining and practicing leadership to grow organizations, improve our systems and give our very best selves. Undoubtedly, the multiplicity of lessons learned cannot be shared in this book. However, I have chosen to illuminate some characteristics and behaviours that can have potentially positive repercussive effects on the individual and society and, yet, some behaviours, if left unchecked, can stifle our growth forever.

Each chapter in this book is referred to as a "Dimension." Within each dimension are "Insights" and rich perspectives of the dimension itself. The dimension of ***Being*** presents nine empowering insights that deal with understanding self with a view to be more mindful of how we treat others. They show how our behaviours and perspectives of life shape and change our leadership. This dimension forces us to question our practices and be deliberate in our approaches to unearth the potential in others. It highlights some uncomfortable but necessary truths, and presents perspectives often not thoroughly interrogated in leadership discussions. The concept "being" refers to *who you are* and highlights the emotional dimension of leadership. Leadership as "being" suggests a radical shift from the traditionally accepted view of leadership as a mechanical, emotionally detached process of "being" in control, ultra-rational and results-driven. It represents a more emotionally intelligent, mindful and connective style of leadership.

The Dimension of *Learning* is intimately connected with that of "Being." It articulates seven transformational insights. Through the process of becoming, we learn some fundamental lessons from how people treat us and how we contribute to that treatment based on how we view and present ourselves to others. This dimension presents some harsh realities and will propel us to make some tough decisions and change the way we do things.

The Dimension of *Doing* weaves in both *Being* and *Learning*, showing that our actions are not necessarily unconscious or haphazard but rather our decisive moves stems from our acceptance of who we are and what we choose to learn and take from our experiences.

With every page is a nugget that can bring personal transformation and you may find that my experiences are not unique, as you too would have had some of them. You may find yourself thinking that you know people who behave like those I have described or that, at some point, you have demonstrated those behaviours yourself. Whatever the connection, the book is meant to offer you a new set of lens on leadership. It will help you negotiate your space, navigate challenges, consciously, and ultimately, build and grow others to improve our world.

Go ahead, turn the pages and enjoy the journey!

DIMENSION 1

LEADERSHIP AS BEING

I am who I am because of everyone.
~ Orange TV advert (2008)

Insight 1: There Is Always A Beginning

I was the first child in my family to attend University. My inclinations to aim high have been with me for as long as I can remember. I believe that such inclinations have opened doors previously unknown to me. With a relentless spirit, in my sixth form years of high school, I moved to a new house seven times in just one year in an effort to find a place to live to avoid travelling about thirty-two miles to school every morning. My house movement was not of my own accord; rather my mother had to find another family after each one that took me in decided I could not stay in their abode anymore. The original plan was to keep me at no boarding fee and my mother would provide my food every week. This plan did not last very long for some of my caregivers. After a while they started to demand money to sustain my stay. My mother felt they had every right to be compensated to keep me, she just could not afford to pay. She was poor, very poor and I have come to understand that she really was the definition of what poor meant in those days.

Back then, all I wanted was a shed and a bed, electricity and water, but all those who agreed to keep me without payment, changed their minds. Some passed out reasons that I studied too much and, therefore, was racking up the electricity bill (even after I begged to stay and decided to study for my tests and exams using the streetlights). That alternative was not enough. They wanted me out. Others wanted me gone after failed attempts at molestation and demoralization. Still others ushered me out after my mother could not fulfill her obligation of finding my food. The ground provision she took every Saturday was, for them, just not enough. Farmers, pastors, business owners, teachers, and even executive heads led some of these homes. I was privileged to interact with them all.

During my university years and the beginning stages of my career, I had opportunities to travel to almost every continent. I have travelled to the point where getting on a plane has become a chore. I have met all kinds of people across various cultures. I have lived with different kinds of families, from the rich and privileged, the superstitious, the obsessed with societal views, to the very poor, very uneducated and unconcerned. I have been led by and have sat at the feet of various kinds of people, bosses and supervisors of differing cultures, convictions and ages. I have studied them, written about them, encouraged them and have been bemused by some. I have not seen it all. There are many veils to part, more doors to open, and still more behind those. When one question is answered, two more emerge. However, I have seen a lot and I have concluded that indeed leadership is the most intriguing expression of human behaviour.

There is nothing more interesting than watching leaders in action. Some sit with their shoulders erect and navigate others through tough decision-making. Some blend into their organizations and motivate others towards innovative, ground-breaking solutions. Others use their strategic planning skills to create a vision that calls for change. Yet some administer responsibilities and exercise authority for incremental improvement. Among the varying views on the radical differences within this one construct, there is one inarguable similarity, one indispensable thread – *people*.

> **There is nothing more interesting than watching leaders in action.**

Leadership cannot exist without people. The people define it, honour it or abhor it. The people give it value, longevity and success. The people make it flourish...or stagnate. Yes, the people are that powerful! However, the question is, "Do leaders really understand that?"

> **Leadership cannot exist without people. The people define it, honour it or abhor it.**

At the age of seventeen, I had my first paying job. It was the summer of my upper sixth form year and the goal was to earn some money to offset my dormitory fee, as I would be starting University the next September and a Student Loan would take care of tuition. I was excited to learn, to talk to new people and to see what the salary would look like. I was just seventeen and I had never been engaged outside of school or church. A job was a new experience and one which proved to be a defining experience. I gained lasting insights and learned formative lessons.

I started my first job as an assistant in a department that processed identification cards for individuals in order to facilitate the payment of their taxes. My job was not very technical; however, it was a job I took seriously.

On the first day, I pulled out my very best attire; a washed-out flowered top I tucked into a grey pencil skirt and flat shoes with stockings. I was going to work and wanted to look smart and responsible. Upon arriving at work, I was introduced to a supervisor who barely looked up at me from her desk. She ushered me off to another colleague, who seemed to be a seasoned employee. That colleague firstly explained the rules of the organization, which were, "no tight clothes," "one hour for lunch," "arrive at 8:30am" and "exit at 4:30pm." She then moved on to explain what I would be responsible for doing on a daily basis, which was, attend to the people who came in and route their concerns where necessary, laminate the identification cards and document the requests and issuance of said cards. Most people in the office area seemed to be rather attached to their desks and detached from everything else. I was like a ghost in that space. Except for one colleague, who quickly explained to me, "the way things are around here." She said, "My dear, just do your work and go home. The boss likes no one and no one likes her, as a matter of fact nobody here likes nobody." I decided to follow the rules and do my work as was communicated. After all, it was just a summer job. I would be out in less than four months and would have fulfilled the goal of earning some money to offset my University costs. In addition, for those three months, the supervisor never spoke to me. I, however, spent those months doing my work but observing and noting slighted experiences, poor customer service, poor work relationships, haughty employees, disengaged team members and a phantom leader whose presence or absence seemed to be of no moment.

That experience cemented in me a habit of observing people in organizations and especially leaders. Every job I had and every opportunity in an office or space with people was marked by observing the leadership and the team's response to the leader. My interest for understanding leadership and leadership behaviours forced me to search for deeper meaning on how and why leaders have such an impact on others, why leaders continue to make so many mistakes and why proven pathways of solutions have been avoided. I wanted to discern the underlying truths of my observations and to figure out how I could fit them together as a whole. This curiosity propelled me to pursue postgraduate education in leadership and leadership development and today, other than being with my family, I spend a lot of time observing and analysing leadership behaviours. There is always a beginning. Something triggers our behaviours. Something is responsible for our actions and reactions. Whatever it may be, we need to find it and understand it because only then can we control ourselves. Becoming self-aware is not only the beginning but also loops and double loops through our entire journey. I now understand who I am and why I do what I do and will continue to do it. I continue to confront my blockages and biases and my actions are not aimless but carefully crafted, seeking for a solution or an explanation.

Insight 2: The Way You See People Is The Way You Lead Them

I have had diverse experiences in my career. I have sat with various supervisors and have noticed fundamental differences in them on my journey. I have recognized too that my own idiosyncrasies as a leader was evolving. Upon reflection, I accord this evolution to the influence of my supervisors over the years. All of them aided in forming who I am today. I have had leaders who have been nothing short of amazing in terms of their skills in dealing with people and I have had some who could, well, benefit greatly from reading this book.

When I took on my first job as young manager in a very large organization, I worked alongside a rather experienced leader whose perception of people was very poor. He had a belief system that he was, by far, the most brilliant person in the organization and that his team members could and should never be above him. He accorded them the same treatment, micromanaging their work, having limited engagement with them, and intimated performance conversations when he was just about ready to ask for their resignation. Mr. Mullings' (my pseudonym) team struggled to grow. He became frustrated easily, complained about how overworked he was and spoke rather negatively about his team to those around him. Mr. Mullings was quite competent, so his organization was able to report positively on its deliverables as he worked tirelessly in the night and on the weekends to organize activities for maximum output.

Mr. Mullings was also determined that he could never look bad to his other colleagues, so he squeezed out all he could from his team members. He pulled on them on their weekends, at odd hours of the night, during their lunchtime and holidays. They produced much but were barely commended, and when they received commendations, it was in a private space between him and the employee and often laced with criticism. Mr. Mullings' team members were disenchanted. He never saw his own behaviour or his treatment towards his colleagues as any variable in their performance. He chanted a philosophy of their lack of personal agency, but never recognised that he did not provide the platform or created the atmosphere for his team to grow. The weak link in the organization was Mr. Mullings. It was affecting what his team was becoming, and he failed to realize it. Yes, the weak link in the organization may just be you. It is tough to admit it, but the quicker you assess the situation, the more time you will have to fix it. The only way your business, school or

> **Strong leaders do not reflect individual talent, they survive on team competencies.**

organization can be great is if you grow talent. You must grow your team members to lead better than you. If you fail to develop a critical mass that is stronger or as strong as you are, you can say goodbye to impact. Strong leaders do not reflect individual talent, they survive on team competencies.

Mr. Mullings did not recognize where he was going wrong and neither do many of us on this leadership journey. Mr. Mullings failed to see that his most fundamental beliefs were becoming evident in his leadership practices. Our speeches, writings, reprimands and approvals are reflections of our heart and mind on leadership. As leaders, we need to understand that team members do not necessarily change us, we change them. We influence their attitude, dispositions and behaviours, whether positively or negatively, by the way we treat them and by the perceptions we have of them. We bring out their distinctive strengths and potentials. We illuminate their failings and lack of competencies. We lead who we are. Our idiosyncrasies and our most intimate thoughts shine through in our leadership. Like the ostrich that buries its head in the sand, we are only fooling ourselves if we believe people do not see straight through us. When we take on leadership roles, we become naked. It becomes

> **When we take on leadership roles, we become naked. It becomes extremely difficult to hide our true selves.**

extremely difficult to hide our true selves. Skills and competencies become secondary and our innermost selves are played out in the tritest and the most challenging of situations.

We, therefore, need to examine how we really see people. It is a perception in many organizations that specialization and division of labour increases efficiency and enhances performance. Structural leaders maintain that organizations operate at their optimal when functions are hierarchical and rules-oriented. These leaders enforce performance and efficiency through hierarchical divides and inflexible rules. Though this approach has its merits, we cannot ignore that hierarchies can create mechanistic environments in which employees can be made to feel like "pawns" – individuals who lack the capability to do things without being directed by authority. The concept of individuals as "pawns" in the work environment was conceptualized by DeCharms (1965). Indeed, this notion is also akin to Pavlov's classical conditioning. Hierarchies can create employees whose behaviours are controlled by external forces – often the voice, look or whim of the leader.

> **When people's perspectives are sought and valued, they feel part of the process, part of the leadership, integral to the organization. They support what they help to create.**

If what characterizes "pawns" is their laziness and lack of creativity based on the leader's evaluations, then, DeCharms affirms "origins" as being self-directed and empowered. Do we want "origins" or "pawns?" The truth is, we can create either of them. "Origins" work with leaders, and not for leaders. When people's perspectives are sought and valued, they feel part of the process, part of the leadership, integral to the organization. They support what they help to create. They are "origins." Interestingly, when people are valued as "origins" they see themselves as co-owners of the organization. They invest valuable time, considerable energy and essential care in ensuring that the organization realizes its goal. It is safe to say that when people are empowered, the organization is assured a competitive advantage.

> It is safe to say that when people are empowered, the organization is assured a competitive advantage.

It is, therefore, critical to examine how leaders operate in organizations; who they are and how they treat people result in what the organization eventually becomes. Excellent organizations are not formed by accident. It requires empowering your team through capacity building, stretch projects, engaging in performance conversations, building relationships, having difficult conversations, saying yes with excitement and no with love, spotting and communicating strengths, building and teaching how to staff weaknesses. All this requires leadership that is confident, informed, open to learning, fearless, compassionate, strategic and visionary. Indeed, we can teach many things, but the only person we can teach others to be is ourselves.

Insight 3: Your Colleagues Are Not Your Competition But Your Reinforcement

We all want to see things change. We all want to be part of something meaningful and we all want to be fulfilled in our jobs. Nobody gets up and goes to work with the intention of messing things up. Our behaviours and dispositions are often screaming one thing, "the need to feel valued, respected and appreciated for what we do." How can these seemingly simple needs be met in an organization? Who has the time or the tenacity to ensure that each worker is being valued, effective behaviours are lauded, ineffective performance is respectfully communicated and strategies for improvement employed? Seriously, whose job is it to be checking organizational temperatures, monitoring and evaluating, visioning, strategizing, anticipating and planning for change? It is much easier to just go to work and focus on our little desks and leave, right? The answer to that is a resounding no. Every member of the organization has a role to play in the ethos of the workplace and the professional well-being of our colleagues. However, it takes a certain kind of leadership to set the pace and shape the culture of the organization for members to see themselves in the big picture.

> **Every member of the organization has a role to play in the ethos of the workplace and the professional well-being of our colleagues.**

I often implore managers to choose the very best people to be on their teams. I tell them to be careful not to recruit themselves, not to replicate their skillsets on the team but rather look for diverse skill sets, the very best and brightest from the pool. I see though that leaders often struggle to do this. I will give you a few reasons why there is a struggle: let us take a General Manager whose qualifications may be at the Masters level but requires a Director as a second in command. As General Manager, you may have apprehensions of employing a PhD holder as your second in command. Truthfully, there may be feelings of inadequacy. There may be feelings that this person will outshine you and topple you for the top job in the organization. Though the skillsets and competencies of the PhD holder may be those required to move the organization to rapid growth, in the selection process you may choose to go a little lower down the line and select the candidate who has the same or a tad bit lower qualification than you do. In addition, this individual may be a bit mediocre, but these mediocre competency levels give you a sense of comfort and control that you are still the best and brightest in the room. You will sooner than later realise the mistake when you are overly stressed with deliverables that are suboptimal or just not met, profits that seize, complaints, complacency and overwhelmingly average performance.

Good leaders hire the best and the superior employees. The leader who has the ability to build a great team will always be an asset to the organization. When your colleagues are doing superior work because you give them the space to do so, they dramatically increase your effectiveness. You see, when people are looking at an organization's performance, they are not looking at, or for, individual team members. They are looking for the leader of the team. Joseph Deitch in his book "Elevate" said, *"A manager who creates high performing teams is generally more valuable than an individual employee who performs one function well."* Recognizing that others bring unique gifts to the table that you as a leader just do not have is critical to how you progress in the leadership journey. Others need to be given a voice and space to show that they can. They need to be trusted to do the work and then recognized for having done it well. No vision can be accomplished without an

> **Good leaders hire the best and the superior employees.**

inner circle; a team of people who are enabled, empowered and entrusted with tasks, strategies and initiatives. It takes a strong sense of security and abundance mind-set to release people, to show them to the world and to stand back and make them take the lead. Contrary to popular thinking, it adds value to you rather than take it away. When your team members are shining, they shine on you and, in turn, your organization is illuminated. The highest priority then must be to develop others so that the success of the organization can be sustained, even when you are not around.

> **When your team members are shining, they shine on you and, in turn, your organization is illuminated.**

Importantly, it requires collaboration and not competition. I have interacted with many young employees who complain that they struggle in their jobs and are consistently devising an exit strategy as the older employees, or even their bosses, feel threatened by them and, as such, refuse to give them opportunities to be innovative or creative. They lament that their work is hidden and, in some cases, re-packaged and presented as belonging to another. Efforts to hide their light are more often exerted than a desire to display their ingenuity and catapult the organization to higher

> **Hiding talent in any shape can only prove crippling to organizations.**

heights. Hiding talent in any shape can only prove crippling to organizations. Each person is equipped with varying skills and competencies uniquely packaged and necessary to advance the workspace.

Younger employees are not to be seen as competition but as reinforcement. What they lack, older generations have, and what older generations lack, they have in abundance. The future requires each mind and each skill set. We cannot do without a wealth of experience and wisdom to provide reassurance, and a seasoned voice that recounts the history that shaped the organization's successes and failures. Neither can we advance without that charismatic personality that empowers; that agile mind that sees ten years in advance and an intellect that creates sustainable systems and processes in record time. The reality is that trading one generation in favour of another can reign no more. We are now living in a boundary-less and borderless world that is driven by pooling the best of each person. There is just too much talent in our people to silence and stifle.

In 1986, Alfie Kohn wrote a book called, "The Case against Competition." He expressed that, *"the simplest way to understand why competition does not generally promote excellence is to realize that trying to do well and trying to beat others are two different things."* We often confuse doing well with competing with another. That mindset must shift in order to get the results we want. A desire to do well is not necessarily aligned with doing better than another, but one that is fixed on raising the bar of whatever you do to a higher standard. You only do well when you have surpassed your own limits, not the limits of another. Your competition should only be yourself as, in that case, you are actively working on advancing to another level. However, I cannot emphasize how success at any level requires working as a team as humans exist in a symbiotic relationship with community. People are dependent on each other and desire mutual trust and collaboration. There will always be a need for collective and interactive efforts to build a community, organization, business, church, home, relationships, and school or just about anything that is sustainable. The route to high performance is fostering collaboration.

> You only do well when you have surpassed your own limits, not the limits of another.

Insight 4: You Are More Than Likely Getting What You Give

In a series of focus group interviews I carried out several years ago to ascertain why the Spanish Language was not embraced as a subject across three institutions, I learned that leaders could become blind to the repercussions of their own practices. In those interviews, the teachers of Spanish expressed that the students did not like the subject. The students expressed that the teachers made the subject boring. They complained that it lacked creativity and play; two elements of teaching not only necessary for the modern languages classroom but also for effective learning in general. The principals of the schools also indicated that they did not see the relevance of the subject and so did not accord it many resources. They, however, were demanding more from both the teachers and the students. They could not see that their leadership behaviour directly affected the outcome.

Flourishing schools too do not just flourish; there are underlying causes. In an interview with a high performing principal of a leading secondary school in Jamaica, the question was asked, "Why do the students do so well?" The principal quipped, "Well, many will say resources, but I know better. Here we allow teachers to think, we celebrate their creativity and we empower their growth. They do the same with their students." The response was unexpected but simple and compelling. The requirement then is that we begin as leaders to interrogate our practices. We need to ask ourselves these questions:

- What am I doing that may be a direct correlation with the response I get from my team?

- Why are my team members silent when I speak?
- Why is there limited feedback?
- Why do people just seem to come in, work and leave and there seems to be little engagement or connectivity?
- Why am I not getting the results that I need?"

These questions are critical starting points to understanding what we may need to do less, what we may need to change totally, what we may need to keep doing or what we may need to start doing in our leadership practices.

It is only when we confront ourselves and begin to get honest about our own approaches that we begin to recognize who we are and, more importantly, who we have been to others. The formula is simple: we lead who we are, and

> **We lead who we are, and what we give to people is what we will most likely get back from them.**

what we give to people is what we will most likely get back from them. As Jawaharlal Nehru, first Prime Minister of independent India stated: *"It is a fundamental rule in life, that if the approach is good, the response is good."* Many leaders, having recognized their own failings and the difficulty of co-existing in leadership spaces in moments of frustration, state that people and situations should be accepted as they are. I have heard statements such as, "I am who I am" or "it is what it is." I, however, submit that for

> leaders to succeed;
> individuals to grow and maximize their full potential;
> visions to be realized;
> organizations to flourish;
> stakeholders to be engaged;
> barriers to be broken down;
> justice to prevail;
> souls to be saved;
> talents to be birthed;
> nations to be built;
> the innocent to be set free;
> children to learn;
> profits to be sustained;
> churches to grow;
> lives to be protected;
> innovations to be unearthed; and
> unchartered territories to be discovered,

we cannot maintain that, "It is what it is" and I cannot continue to say, "I am who I am." We MUST seek to change. We must seek to do better, to do differently; otherwise, we end up in a perpetual flux of desiring a different state that no one but ourselves have the power to create. Dealing with our weaknesses then becomes an imperative. To achieve the goals we want in our spiritual, personal and professional lives, we must confront our failings. We do this by changing our perceptions of people and situations. You see, it is our perceptions of people and situations that cause us to act the way we do and to react with aggression or calmness. If we begin to see people for who they can become rather than who they are, we begin to see potential, capabilities and beauty. We begin to see them through God's eyes; the same way He sees us. This becomes the beginning; the starting point to dealing with our weaknesses.

> To achieve the goals we want in our spiritual, personal and professional lives, we must confront our failings.

Insight 5: We Grow Talent By Delegating, Not Dumping

Every leader will undoubtedly have team members who have deficiencies that can damage their organization. At some point, we are faced with the decision of letting people go, retaining them or developing them. Certainly, there are times when letting people go is the very best option and may very well be the best decision. However, if our proclivity is to "let go" then it means we have not tapped into the most fundamental aspect of leadership; that of developing others. To develop others, we must see beyond their deficiencies; see what they can become. Now this is a purposeful way of operating. We must become serious about seeing beyond deficiencies and proactive about working with individuals to bring to light their strengths. Bringing light to strength can best be achieved through purposeful mentoring or delegating.

> **We must become serious about seeing beyond deficiencies and proactive about working with individuals to bring to light their strengths.**

Delegation matters in the growth experience. However, sometimes we may mistake behaviours of dumping with those of delegation. Dumping is laziness and injustice to others on the leadership journey. Dumping is throwing unwanted work on colleagues or passing on work that we have failed to do because of our deficiencies or lack of structure in an organization.

Delegation is one method that is used to illuminate strengths. It is purposeful and proactive. When we delegate, we recognize a strength that can be enhanced or we spot an opportunity for development. We place our colleagues to work in areas that will positively challenge them to advance to greater levels of competence. For example, our absence from work should provide opportunities for delegation, introduction of new projects, improvement of systems and processes; stakeholder building and engagement should propel us to actively devise a plan to challenge team members. Delegation requires a three-step process. These are identification, implementation and evaluation.

Step 1: The Identifying Stage

The identifying stage is spotting the potential for illumination. This is the stage where we articulate to our colleagues the talents and capabilities they have that have generative power. Often these may be strengths that are underutilized or unrecognized to those who possess them. They are often waiting to be tapped. It is the responsibility of leadership to shine strengths on the potential of their team members and to let them know who they can become. The implementation stage is one that requires the leader to provide support to the team member. It is not a time for us to watch and wait to see if the tasks we have given will be accomplished the way we want them to. Rather, we should guide, mentor, coach and continue to check in to ensure that things are on target. This is true delegation. When we do this, we create a powerfully positive presence that our team members will be drawn to follow. We also get an opportunity to see unique capabilities in this guiding stage as people become comfortable with being vulnerable when they recognise that they are genuinely supported and there is a desire that they succeed.

Step 2: The Implementation Stage

The implementation stage requires engaging and encouraging, rather than mandating and manipulating. Seeing and valuing the team members' skills and aspirations will yield great outcomes and lead to high-level performance that others can replicate.

Step 3: The Evaluation Stage

The final stage is the evaluation stage. At this stage, leaders must engage in authentic performance conversations. Sometimes, this can prove challenging and we find that it is not in our nature to be blatantly honest to people about their performance – especially if the person is weak. Nevertheless, the goal of delegation is not met without the performance conversation. Having performance conversations is an indispensable practice that will unleash the capabilities vested in this multi-generational and multi-talented workforce. Individuals deserve to be made aware of how they are doing and what we think they may be doing well or otherwise.

> **The goal of delegation is not met without the performance conversation.**

It is the time to communicate and engage the team members about how they managed the task or project. The more open we are in illuminating what they did that was useful, relevant, revolutionary, traditional, substandard, average or mediocre, the more they grow and learn to do and become better. We cement and raise the standards through the performance conversations, and we inadvertently teach others how to evaluate their own work and validate themselves. Let us remember that we lead who we are and so the more we practice engaging approaches, the more engaging we will become.

Insight 6: Power Is Not Leadership

Indeed, for some among us, it is an exhilarating feeling to be in control. I once heard a Business Owner speaking about his love for power and quite unabashedly too. He articulated that not knowing and dictating what happens when and where inside his office made him feel handicapped. Nothing should catch him by surprise. His desire to be omnipotent made it extremely difficult for his team to plan anything for him. There could be no surprise birthday party in his honour, no surprise awards ceremony validating his leadership, no surprise lunch or sporadic meeting. He had to know

> **Leadership from time immemorial has been associated with power.**

and decide everything. The pleasure of dominating was his driving force everyday. Whilst power is a necessary piece of the leadership puzzle, they are not one and the same. Power is the ability or the capacity to get that which you want, when you want it and prevent outcomes that are against your wishes; the ability to grant favours or to withhold support, to deny and to delay. It often stems from an institutional position or having great influence on one that holds an institutional position. Leadership from time immemorial has been associated with power. The power concept may be so dominant because of man's innate desire to be in control.

Structural theorists position authorities as ultimate sources of power (Bolman and Deal, 2003). I have observed many structural organizations wherein power is a commodity best achieved and kept through coercion, manipulation and deceit. Leaders, therefore, display characteristics that are cold, calculative and crafty. In my observation of decision-making in these structural organizations, the administrators often made decisions ahead of time and the verdict handed down in a *Memorandum*. However, in order to project an image of dialogical relations among team members in the decision-making process, they would convene meetings informing of issues to be discussed. After the monologues and soliloquies, one could most certainly expect the following question punctuated with a smile: "Do these work for you?" but before a response is accepted, a firm statement such as this would follow: "It is the best thing to do given the circumstances." All would then nod in acceptance of the decisions with a false sense of satisfaction that they helped in making them. And, yet, there are others who do not consult on the basis that they are in charge and so decisions are made for us and not by us. This kind of dramaturgy, perhaps then, was not something I realised, but upon reflection conclude that employees in those organizations were controlled by the wielding sword of authoritative power.

Displaying Power Through Communication

I have heard the lamentations of many employees on how distressed they are with the way their bosses speak to them. "She speaks down to me," they say. "He speaks to me as if I have no sense," they complain. "She speaks to me as if I am her child," others relate. Yes, communication is a form of power play. Sometimes leaders use the tone of their voice to move their employees into submission or to create an atmosphere of control. Communication should never be practiced as a parent-child relationship. Leaders in organizations are not parents of colleagues or team members. They, therefore, should not speak to them

> **Communication should never be practiced as a parent-child relationship.**

as such. The highest degree of respect is expected from both leaders and followers and respect is only consistently reciprocated if it is given. These kinds of power play do not serve to strengthen one's hold on individuals. People may respond in fear of losing their jobs or being slighted for promotion but deep down their respect for the leader is eroded and the moment they get an opportunity where the leader has no influence over them, they show their true feelings and react quite authentically.

Winston Churchill communicated that: *"Dictators ride to and fro upon tigers from which they dare not dismount, and the tigers are getting hungry."* Indeed, when you lead from a position of power, you must work thrice as hard to keep that position. The moment you are dismounted, discarded or debased is the moment the people will act like a volcanic force to ensure you never get another leadership opportunity.

Sharing Power

Contra-wise to the structural theory, recent studies on power proves that power is most effective when it is shared. The notion of power as shared does not regard power as inherent in people or positions but more so as existing in relationships. The human resource frame stresses that power is neither a commodity nor a social construct divorced from human actions. Power is more effective through collaboration and mutuality. Sharing power in an organization means sharing leadership roles. The idea of shared leadership signifies that many more people than the designated leaders have the information and the power to make decisions and enact changes.

This paradox of power is evident in the human resource prism. Human resource theorists emphasize that the more power leaders give workers to act upon initiatives and exercise freedom and individuality, the more power the leader gains. Essentially, the more power that is shared in the organization, the more workers give back to the organization. For example, in a school where teachers are given power to design and refine the curriculum, and teachers along with administrators create the staff handbook, the collaborative process of creating documents of rules and guidelines that govern conduct as well as the teaching-learning experience will allow teachers to feel a sense of worth and appreciation. Shared leadership is advantageous both to the individual and to the organization because issues can become complex in organizational dynamics. In complex situations, a

> **Shared leadership is advantageous both to the individual and to the organization because issues can become complex in organizational dynamics.**

human resource perspective allows more than one mind to clarify, analyze and respond to these issues. Leaders must be careful not to project leadership as a function embedded in one person, but as a function to be performed within a group in helping the group to grow and to work productively.

The *man at the top* approach, as flaunted by trait theorists, permeates the leadership practice, though the vast literature on leadership and leadership development illuminates the flaws and potentially destructive and debilitating organizational structures that hold true to that perspective. However, leadership ought not to be viewed or practiced as power over people but as power over systems, structures, resources, concepts and situations. Individuals in an organization come with multiple skills and perspectives from other roles and life experiences and, therefore, have a workable solution to an organization's perennial problems. Sharing power allows for solutions and when problems are solved, organizations grow and, doubtless, the designated leaders shine.

> **Leadership ought not to be viewed or practiced as power over people but as power over systems, structures, resources, concepts and situations.**

Insight 7: Nothing Needs To Be In It For You

The leadership journey in its truest sense is one that is marked by unselfishness. The journey to successful leadership is one that eradicates competition and focuses on a fight that is bigger than one is. Competition suggest fighting for a cause; for "me"; collaboration suggests fighting for a cause; for "us"; a greater good that cannot happen on any solo act. True leaders act on motives that are not related to fulfilling their own desires.

> **True leaders act on motives that are not related to fulfilling their own desires.**

Early in my study at the University of Saskatchewan, I was privileged to interview and communicate with Simone (as part of my dissertation), a student from Iran, who came to Canada as an immigrant and was studying at the University and excelling in student leadership. Simone related the internal conflict that she had within herself when she was campaigning for her post on the Student Leadership Executive of the University. She expressed that she felt that her campaign was a selfish act. She related her inner turmoil of questioning herself and trying to find a motive that was not related to fulfilling her own desires. She referred to that period as a "conflict of interest" within herself because she knew she wanted to help but she also knew that her campaign, at that time, was not related to wanting to help but to fulfilling her own selfish leadership desires. She expressed that feeling engaged in her leadership happened when she identified a cause that had nothing to do with her, but one that was related to the greater good of the wider student population. She said:

I was leading the [travel mode poll] (my pseudonym) last year, so I hope you are not mad that it passed because that was my effort. Anyway, I really believed in it and I believed in it for multiple reasons. I feel very deeply about my city. I feel deeply about my country. Climate change is affecting us and so getting a bus-pass is a good thing. Plus, for students who cannot afford a regular [travel ticket] this is important. I just got my car a couple days ago, because I could not afford to have a car and a [travel ticket]. But what engaged me the most is that other people wanted it, so I wasn't speaking for myself and what I wanted but I also knew that I had 600 people who signed this petition that wanted it. I found that it was just so much easier to argue with someone, try to convince another or just have dialogue about an issue that was bigger than me; that I knew more people wanted. It is different from when I was campaigning for this position. During that time, I felt like it was so personal and that it was really hard to say to someone, "You should vote for me because I was this and that." I felt like it was all about me. Therefore, I struggled with it. I kept on asking myself, "Why should I vote for me?" Is it because I would like the position or because I think I could be good for others? How do I know what other people want? It was like a conflict of interest within me. Whereas, with the bus-pass, it was very clear. Getting the bus-pass for all students accepted by the University was not for me. I knew for sure I was helping people. I knew it was not selfish, so I felt deeply engaged because it was more than just something I wanted for myself (Ingleton, 2014).

One binding element in Simone's perspective about leadership is that leadership is essentially serving others. Simone understood that she, as an individual, was not very important. The story she related suggested that she felt that pursuing her own desires was not emotionally satisfying for her, neither would it resonate with others around her. For Simone, unless she could identify that definite cause, one from which she was not necessarily gaining, then her service was disingenuous.

Simone ended her story by saying, "It was more than just something I wanted for myself." Paradoxically, it was by exclusion of self that Simone felt most engaged. It was by taking herself out of the story that she became embraced within the wider story. Simone espoused a civic-minded philosophy. She believed in people, and in serving their needs. She experienced a subjection of her own desires as well as a conscious decision and a compelling passion to serve the best interest and needs of the people she was leading.

Leadership happens when we release the passion of our service towards others. It is accomplishing the superior together, not making another feel inferior. Simone may, unfortunately, be a rare kind. This is a world driven by competition and persons obsessed with the desire for recognition, promotion and influence. The *Simones* of this day are needed. They are needed to create pride in citizens, passion in students, understanding in our youth, justice in our courts, wellness in our patients, integrity in our politicians, truth in our churches, honour in our homes, wisdom in our elders, trust in our relationships and value for our customers. We really do not need to act because we have something to gain or lose. Acting without any self-interest ought to be a leadership rhetoric and a foundational dimension of the practice and principle of leadership.

> **Leadership happens when we release the passion of our service towards others.**

Insight 8: It Requires Strength To Be Compassionate

Leaders who cry, smile often, speak positively in the life of the team, and express empathy in challenging situations are sometimes viewed as weak. Strength in leadership has been misinterpreted for being unfeeling, sword-wielding, aggressive and participating in uncompromising acts that drive fear into people and compel them to perform. However, we are seeing more and more each day that these leadership behaviours are not sustainable, and they do not build strong organizations. People will react either passively or aggressively. For the passive, there is silence, apathy, absence, mediocrity and mass exodus from the organization. For the aggressive, there are acts of sabotage, campaigns against policies, insubordination and mass exodus from the organization.

In my interview with Simone, she saw expressions of compassion as being "in tune" with the feelings of others. She expressed that her ability to show sincere, heartfelt consideration for those whom she served made her more attentive to the needs of others in her leadership practices. She related, "You can't have hard work, if you don't have compassion; you can't be dedicated, if you don't care." Simone seamlessly expressed how she willingly brings the basic human emotion into her role, how she expresses vulnerability and, by doing so, communicates more effectively. She expressed that brokenness affected her and when it did, she cried uncontrollably with people. Simone said:

When I look back, I would say that expressing compassion helped a lot in my leadership. So [this girl] moved here and she is from a very liberal family. So, for example, when you are born in [a country where Muslim is the primary religion] you are forced to declare that you are a Muslim or else your life may be terminated. Therefore, she is sitting in my office crying, because she is living with her brother and his wife. The wife does not want her [at their house] anymore. She needs to find housing. She has been waiting since January to get into housing [in one of the university residences]. No one is giving her straight answers. It is just ridiculous. And something terrible happened to her. Now, between you and me, you can probably imagine what happened to her. In addition, I am trying so hard to hold back my tears. She is not wearing a veil; she has arms and ankles showing, and I am like, so do you think that is why your brother's wife want you gone, because she is more traditional than you are? I tried so hard and finally got her housing but I was crying with her and I was saying to myself "am not gonna make a good leader if I keep crying with people." But I just couldn't stop. Then she emailed me after she got the housing and told me that no one ever treated her like a real person, except for me. See, I am crying now just thinking about it. She invited me to her dormitory for dinner and showed me pictures of her and her friends back [home] wearing short dresses and drinking booze. On the outside, they would be wearing scarfs and jeans. This was emotional for me because I felt like I connected with her on a very personal level (Ingleton, 2014).

Simone's deep feelings of compassion for individuals was what she thought brought life to her leadership. Her comments suggested that she led with her heart and understood that people are, at first, humans. Simone's willingness to express herself through crying with this individual caused her to be perceived as a person for whom someone now had great respect instead of a weak person. Simone had a deep understanding of this young girl's emotional state. Her statement, "I felt like I connected with her on a very personal level" evidences this.

Compassion and leadership are not incongruent, but two pieces that fit perfectly together. A leader's compassion is not a mere emotional response but a commitment to action. Once you feel, you are compelled to do. I often cry with my colleagues and for them. What they feel, I feel. Injustice, unfair treatment and lack of regard gets me very sensitive. I used to believe that it was a weakness. In fact, I was told I needed to drop my emotions and toughen up. My sensitivity to people's hurt brought me embarrassing moments where I ended up struggling with myself and questioning my own growth and maturity. I was thinking I should not be feeling so much for others. Something must be wrong with me. I remember crying so hard for a colleague who my supervisor had determined to terminate. I felt her pain, her fear and anxiety of not knowing what will happen next. I remember engaging him about

> **Compassion and leadership are not incongruent, but two pieces that fit perfectly together.**

the need to be fair, just, and compassionate. Certainly, he laughed at my emotions for her, thinking I was too weak. I convinced him to keep her on the team and give her time to grow. He did and I have lived to see that young woman blossom into a confident and powerful professional in her career and I smile every time I see her. To date, he sees her as one of the best team members he has ever experienced.

Leaders must be able to see through the eyes of another. We must be able to understand the hearts we speak into. Charismatic speeches, promises and policies are not enough. Our constituents look out for our deeds. They expect us to show up, pay attention and do something regardless of the situation. There is no other way to show that you are deeply committed to the aspiration you espouse. Credibility in leadership is not gained through qualifications, the power of your network or years of experience, but in consistently responding, feeling and doing that which you said you would do. There must be consonance with your words and actions.

> **Credibility in leadership is not gained through qualifications, the power of your network or years of experience, but in consistently responding, feeling and doing that which you said you would do.**

Insight 9: Praise Elevates

It is a desire of every human being to be commended for a job well done. The desire for commendation surpasses age, race, gender and stages of development. Feelings of worth and value, or the lack thereof, are perpetuated in work and school settings because of the potentially positive repercussive benefits. Dale Carnegie (1964) wrote that a key to winning friends and influencing people is to *"be hearty in your approbation and lavish in your praise."* In schools, behavioral theorists indicate that praising a specific behaviour causes the behaviour to be repeated. Henderlong and Lepper (2002), in their article, *"The Effects of Praise on Children's Intrinsic Motivation: A Review and Synthesis"* argue that:

> *...the potential power of praise is evident in the behavior modification literature, in which programs are developed that involve the systematic and contingent use of praise over time for the purpose of reducing classroom behavior problems and encouraging students to learn. Such work has shown that praise can be a successful technique for influencing a variety of classroom behaviors, from abiding by classroom rules and engaging in positive peer relations, to paying attention to teacher instructions and developing academic skills.*

> **It is a desire of every human being to be commended for a job well done.**

I submit that the effects of praise on adults in an organization do not necessarily differ. When we offer commendation on work approaches, quality of deliverables, attire or attitude, the recipient feels empowered to continue to impress and do better or more. Praise illuminates strengths and when strengths are illuminated, there can only be potential for individuals to get stronger. There are several benefits of praise, but key among them is that it gives renewed energy and encourages divergent thinking. Team members who work hard are often extremely focussed on their outputs and may fall into a routine of hitting high points but not necessarily changing their approaches or finding innovative ways of doing old things. Offering praise to these high performing employees gives a sense of reassurance and further boosts their confidence to examine more challenging approaches or take on more difficult tasks. Making praise a habit in organizations and incorporating it in leadership approaches is critical to creating and sustaining a positive work environment.

> **Praise illuminates strengths and when strengths are illuminated, there can only be potential for individuals to get stronger.**

As my story shows, just a little bit over thirty years of age, with limited experience in designing competency frameworks, but highly passionate about leadership and leadership development and the capabilities of people in organizations, I boldly applied for a job as a consultant to work on a leading project in the Public Service to develop competencies and build on the potential of the Jamaican workforce. Being positive and forceful in the interview, I was selected and at my first meeting was thoroughly commended for an excellent interview and was assured of the confidence the CEO had in me to do very well in the role. It was that commendation and those that followed that gave me impetus to want to do more and exceed her expectations. Her affirmation created a spiral of achievement, which expanded the project and engaged members of the public service in such a positive way and that paved the way for a successful implementation of the project. It should never be doubted that every person in an organization has unique strengths and talents waiting to be unearthed and waiting to be maximised. Positive affirmation and praise will not only facilitate the development of these strengths but can add value to your organization.

> **It should never be doubted that every person in an organization has unique strengths and talents waiting to be unearthed and waiting to be maximised.**

Reflecting On The Being Dimension

The dimension of *"Being"* illuminates who we are at the core. Understanding our limitations, inclinations, and idiosyncrasies is critical to how we grow. It is necessary to examine our triggers, think about those who have influenced us and be ever so sensitive to our biases. Failure to do these things will cause us to lose the trust or confidence our colleagues may have in us. Neglect of the emotional dimension will create myopic interpretations, causing us not to pay attention and prevents us from exercising the wisdom we possess. This can be detrimental to us. But more so, it can be catastrophic to others. Let us never underestimate the world we create when we fail to tap into the feelings of others. Let us not believe that we are not intimately involved in the creation of another's perspective. We are all linked in this web of creation and we ultimately affect each other. That colleague we neglected, that student we mistreated, the employee we rejected and that customer we misjudged is part of the communities we form. All these people become ultimately involved in the policies made, the families we grow and the world we have no choice but to inhabit.

> **We are all linked in this web of creation and we ultimately affect each other.**

Once we embrace and understand the dimension of being, we begin to see perspectives, judge a little less and listen a whole lot more. Learning starts to happen as the "being" dimension encapsulates the reflective and reflexive processes in which we engage. We also start to do things differently, more confidently and more purposefully. Leadership takes on a new form. There is more connectivity and the heart - the most critical part of us - becomes engaged in what we do. It is only then that we will experience authenticity, reject duplicity and lead from a place of courage.

You can use the following questions to engage in a reflection and deep inner dialogue. The response to these questions will help you learn more about yourself and help you begin to tap into the emotional dimension of leadership. Remember, the first and most critical step is to know and understand who you are.

a) Reflect on the people who influenced your leadership. Write down the ones who left a positive impact. Write down as many things they did that made you qualify them as being positive. How much of those behaviours do you now model?

b) Write down the ones you do not admire. Write down as many things they did that cause you not to admire them. How much of those behaviours do you now model?

c) Do you do what you say in every situation?
d) Do you make a decision with your team and then change it behind their backs without explaining?
e) Do you show respect to your colleagues?
f) Do you feel a need to compete with your colleagues?
g) Do you consider crying and other expressions of emotions as a weakness in your leadership or in the leadership of others?
h) Do you validate publicly the work of your colleagues?
i) Do you give credit to the work of others?
j) Do you feel just fine not being in control all the time?

DIMENSION 2

LEADERSHIP AS LEARNING

For a great and effective door is opened unto me, and there are many adversaries.

~ 1 Corinthians 16 vs 9

Learning is a choice, but experiences are inevitable. Many leaders have diverse opportunities by virtue of the portfolios they manage on a daily basis throughout their careers, but only a few really learn. Leadership as learning refers to constantly searching for better outcomes, trying to understand the perspectives, thoughts and behaviours of others, and engaging in a reflective process to improve one's leadership. Learning is a process of acquiring new knowledge as well as reinforcing existing knowledge, which results in a change in behaviour. The struggles you face on the leadership journey are to equip you to lead at higher levels. Every level of opposition you face prepares you for a new dimension of leadership. As difficult as it may seem to understand, one cannot really learn to lead well without opposition, hardship or dissent. These challenges serve to build character, test your moral fortitude, stretch your thinking, positively shift your mindset and cause you to recognize the strength you possess. The lowest periods are the most illuminating and serve to build us up for greater things to come. They should, therefore, be embraced and navigated wisely.

> **The struggles you face on the leadership journey are to equip you to lead at higher levels.**

Insight 10: Learning Through Being Slighted

A turning point in my life as a leader was learning to live and lead without recognition. Indeed, this is a tough one. Who doesn't want to be recognized for a job well done? Who doesn't want to hear thank you? Who doesn't want a reassuring nod or a pat on the shoulder? Who doesn't want to be complimented for their efforts? Who wants to do the job and then someone else gets the credit? As great as we are, as humble as we pretend to be, as righteous as we may portray ourselves, as shy as we may purport, living without recognition is difficult.

I remember vividly in my second year at University, a course on Philosophy that was close to my heart. The course was Philosophy of Mind. We were introduced to the philosopher "René Descartes." I was totally absorbed by Rene Descartes. His perspectives on the relationship between mind and body, our subconscious nature, and the view that mental effects are physical captivated me. It was then that I became a real thinker. Descartes became a part of me, and I took great pleasure in analyzing aspects of his philosophy to my professor and friends. I was Descartes. I made every effort to understand him. I always found a way to include him in my daily conversations. Everyone knew how much I loved and talked about this philosopher. In my Philosophy class, I was the guru on Dualism. However, on the term exam, the professor wrote a quote on Cartesian Dualism and a comment on the quote and indicated on the paper in the exam that this comment was said by another student of the class. The instructions were to analyze the student's (the student's name was there) comment in relation to Descartes' quote. When I saw the quote, my chest tightened. It was my quote. I was only eighteen years old. "That was my comment," I thought. "I said that, and he knows I did. How could he? Everyone knows I said that," I grumbled. "Will no one defend me," I pondered. As I sat there, teary-eyed and desperate for justice, I looked around the lecture theatre and everyone was busy writing the exam. No one seemed to care who said what. They all just wanted to complete that exam paper. No one would rise to my defense.

I did the exam, but with a heart filled with sorrow. I noticed as well that at the end of the exam, no one commented on the error of whose comment it was…no one. I remember that feeling. I doubt anyone remembered it. I have never spoken of it. But it has been my backward embrace to helping and understanding others who have been slighted.

Having this example in my catalogue of experiences, I have become more alert to the feelings of others. I observe the look on their faces. I examine their gestures. I listen to their silence. Being slighted is difficult.

How do we rise from a slighted experience? Do we wallow in self-pity? Do we speak ill of others? Do we withdraw our support for the cause? Do we lose energy and vigour and become someone we are not? Do we move on to other places? Do we pretend we are fine and engage in the hypocrisy? The answer to any of the above questions will determine your strength of character. Eleanor Roosevelt said: *"One's philosophy is not best expressed in words; it is expressed in the choices one makes. In the long run, we shape our lives and we shape ourselves."*

Being slighted is difficult, but we can deal with it and rise gracefully from it, if we come to understand that achievement is who we are and not what we do. Dealing with it gracefully is a skill that can only be learned from experience and intentional efforts. You see, this is a fundamental aspect of leadership that is often unexamined. It is not so much the fireworks that people see but the personal pains that we must learn to endure.

We may never be able to change the world. We may never be able to annihilate the oppressors, but we have unlimited power to change ourselves and to live life to the fullest. You see, the people who know that they are undeserving know that they are undeserving, but their focus is more on the outside than on the inside. In my own observations, reflections and conversations with scores of people who have been slighted, I have learned the following lessons:

a) ***Exert efforts on being better on the inside.*** Indeed, it is natural to be focused on what other people see. It is natural to want to have the glory of men, but it is in no way fulfilling if our hearts are impure. Our reputation comes from what people see. Our character comes from who we are in our private places, in the stillness of the moment and what we do to others who we know cannot affect us. The reputation is the eulogy being read at our deaths. The character is the silent whispers in the church and at the graveside. You choose!

b) ***People matter.*** Making a conscious effort ourselves not to slight others is important. John Maxwell has a simple rule of thumb. It reads: *"Ask yourself what you want people to do for you, then grab the initiative and do it for them."* This is similar to the charge Jesus gave: *"Do unto others as you would have them do unto you."* Relationships are symbiotic and asymmetrical in nature. This life is a contact zone and, at the end of the day, we only add or take away from others. You choose!

c) ***Be authentic.*** There is no one more admirable than a "real" person. As a matter of fact, I believe that the more lasting and most remembered leaders are those who display authenticity; all others will fade away. Talk about, support, enforce and teach only what you believe. Borrowed beliefs or speeches for the moment will be forgotten. Authenticity will make you shine, even in the darkest of places. You may not be liked, you may not climb the career ladder, but you will be remembered and respected. You choose!

Indeed, I am blessed to have seen some good examples. I am blessed to have recognized from an early stage the power of observation and reflection. I am blessed to have learnt the benefits of tension and dissonance. I too have chosen. I have chosen to be purposeful in valuing, believing, affirming, encouraging, motivating, and giving due credit to others. Those who drink the water must never forget those who dug the well.

Learning from our experiences is the most valuable leadership lesson. However, as indicated earlier, learning is a choice.

Insight 11: Learning To Leverage Your Youth

At some point in our lives, we face pain. Pain comes in many forms; some emotional and some physical. The focus of this section is on emotional pain and how we can use it to leverage our leadership. Some of us face the pain of immaturity, the pain of fear, the pain of conflict and even the pain of bad decisions. Yes, all these serve us a hard blow, weaken our morale and cripple our energies. If we are not careful, we many never recover and may continue through life with bitter feelings and warped perceptions of people and the world. Examined differently, pain, of whatever kind, provides us with content and we do not get content without getting things wrong. Content is needed to motivate others and build strength, and it also serves as reflective tools when life gets a little rugged.

I want to share a story of emotional pain I went through in the earlier years of my career. I was often described as "young," "too young" or "young but very talented." I was working in an organization where more than half the people were at least fifteen years my senior. One day, as I was headed down the stairs from a meeting, a colleague stopped me to introduce me to a friend. She referred to me in the introduction as a "child with big qualifications." The person whom she introduced me to looked me up and down and confirmed by the raising of her eyebrows that indeed, I was a child with big qualifications. For years, my physical stature bothered me as individuals would open a statement by referring to me as "little girl," "baby girl" or "young girl." I would burn with anger and my faculties would cry out for self-control, as I was quick to retort with the statement, "I may look young, but I am not a child." My responses were almost always visceral, emotional reactions and I started to wonder why. I started to note my own reactions to the utterance of others of my youth. My reactions were simply marked by fear; fear of desires that may never be met; perceptions that may be unfounded, and dreams that may never come to fruition. I feared being young and was subconsciously equating competence with age and physical stature.

I also suffered through the fear of sharing my ideas as often they were not embraced publicly but ignored or deconstructed to nothingness. I feared advancing anything to the team or my colleagues, which I thought was high level or innovative. I would deliberately water down my ideas or presented them as not original, with the hope that they would be accepted. This season lasted for a while, as no matter how mature and well-tailored my suits and dresses would look (and I would deliberately search for clothes that made me look ten years older), I still physically looked rather young. My youth became a sore point for me at almost every turn and the fear grew to the point where I became miserable and desperate.

When an opportunity for promotion was presented, though I was qualified and competent as demonstrated in my deliverables and feedback on performance appraisals, a senior manager summoned me in her office to encourage me not to apply saying I was too young and should wait my turn. Never mind the leader of the organization was a male and just four years older than me. Her discussion on the matter of the next top-level leadership in the organization was not about my capabilities, skills or competencies, in fact, she admitted that I possessed all that was needed, but I was just too young and should wait.

Her words affected me for days as I painfully watched the time running out to submit the application for the job. I cried in my bathroom, on my way to work, on my way home. I cried to my husband and I cried to my God. I asked, "When will I look 'old' enough to advance in this place?" The answer was "never." In private places, individuals would laud my work and send me private messages as to my excellence, influence and achievements. However, these same individuals would become ridiculously quiet in the meeting room or any public interface where I made a presentation or articulated an idea. It was painful.

The Value Of My Pain

It took me a while, but I started to recognise that my youth was their problem and not mine. My youth was theirs to fear, theirs to stifle but mine to illuminate and to leverage as a strength. I would never be old enough for them. My youth was a mountain they thought they needed to remove for their own advancement and sustainability. I had to learn to use my youth as a strength, as a force, as a way for others in my position to see that they too can rise and make meaningful contributions. I used my pain to grow my capacity for awareness and to loosen my death grip on the opinions and beliefs of others. I had to learn to strategize and market my youth and embrace it, shout it, write about it and illuminate it as the elephant in the room. I had to learn, and I had to learn quickly as every day it seemed as if I was aging backwards.

I started to use my youth to introduce myself and to smile about it. It became an emblem, a significant part of who I was, and a catalytic approach to my marketing plan. I started to embrace other young people, communicated with them, employed them and stretched their thinking. When I speak, my confidence would catch older people by surprise because it was hard to reconcile what they expected with what they were seeing and hearing. I had to use the same thing they were trying to kill as a tool to survive. That is what pain does. It provides opportunities and builds tenacity. I could have chosen to fall prey to that pain and lock myself away, hoping to become old and certainly by that time would have lost such self-confidence; I would have become irrelevant.

My pain contributed to my emotional growth and maturity. It exposed my weaknesses and challenged me to develop my strengths. It made me think harder. It made me search for the gaps in my own work, appearance, rhetoric and leadership. You see, we should never let our pain go to waste. We should use those moments of pressure and feelings of insignificance to learn how to become and do better. We should flip adversity to our advantage. God gives our physical stature to us. We are made in the likeness of His image. He is not unfair, racist, sexist or discriminatory. It, therefore, means that there is purpose in your appearance, and you should use it to magnify God. He has given you your physical stature, hair texture, skin colour and tone of voice to set you apart and help you to live out your true purpose. Developing the right attitude and understanding the power of the learning experience will make you come out of trials as pure gold. Dissenting voices, oppositions, rivals and saboteurs are real gifts. They are all part of the training package to building our fortitude to lead and live well. Job 23 vs 10 says: *"But he knoweth the way that I take: when he hath tried me, I shall come forth as gold."*

Start seeing opponents not as what they can and have done to you, but for what they can do for you. Your critics are your sponsors to help you to operate at a higher level. They inadvertently give you wisdom you could not otherwise pay for or recognize that you even needed.

> **Your critics are your sponsors to help you to operate at a higher level.**

Though my youthful appearance is still a topic for discussion among those who have their own insecurities, it does not affect me anymore. That was the liberation I needed. It does not matter what others may think or believe. We have little control over the convictions of others. What is important is that we do not allow ourselves to become demotivated and crippled by the way people project us. We must learn that there are some things that are not worth our time and energies. Examine the motives of others and see the good and the bad in what they are articulating. Prioritize building on our repertoire of competencies so that we can do better in our work. The focus must always be for us to improve ourselves. It must never be for us to place limitations on our capabilities or to consider our work unworthy.

> **Prioritize building on our repertoire of competencies so that we can do better in our work.**

Another person's criticism should not necessarily be shunned but should be used as a learning tool to give us perspective and to reintroduce us to ourselves. Guard against putting up a brick wall, running away or seeking the next exit. Samuel Lover, the great novelist, once wrote that: *"circumstances are the rulers of the weak; but they are the instruments of the wise."* Good management of pain and bad experiences will prove catalytic to our growth. If we crumble under the pressure, we simply crumble.

Insight 12: There Is Beauty In Ignoring: Learn To Master It

The most difficult skill for me to learn, other than riding a bicycle, which I still cannot ride, was that of ignoring comments, actions and perspectives of others. I always felt that I had to interrogate everything, take everything seriously and give each perspective worth. I have, however, learned that I was only killing myself slowly by doing that. As leaders, we must learn the art of ignoring. The other side of ignoring is focusing. I particularly like the dictionary meaning of ignore which is to "disregard intentionally." This tells me that we must be active and well engaged in order to disengage from others. The activity of ignoring is not passive but purposeful, powerful and necessary. We cannot truly focus unless we are ignoring something or someone that is trying to get our attention. The meaning of focus is to "pay particular attention to." This too is an active process, which requires deliberately refusing to engage with another person or another thing other than that which is of interest to you.

The story of Nehemiah demonstrates this perfectly. Nehemiah had to purposefully ignore Sanballat and Tobias, whose only motive was to distract him from the work he was doing. The message that Nehemiah sent them, after they kept sending word to keep him away from his purpose was: *"I am doing a great work, so that I cannot come down: why should the work cease, whilst I leave it, and come down to you? (Nehemiah 6 vs 3b).* If we do not learn to ignore, we will find that issues we really did not need to deal with will sully our leadership. When our energies are drained, we lose focus and step out of our purpose. Ignoring is like decluttering; getting rid of the unwanted stuff that makes your home look less than beautiful and inviting. To build on great ideas, to excel at tasks, to lead change, to make a meaningful difference requires that we ignore. Indeed, I have learned that there is much beauty in it and so much value to such a skill often not discussed.

The more adept we are at ignoring, is the more tuned in we are to focus on what really matters. The time may not be right to take on a task. We may not be in the right position to argue a point. The network may not be tight or connected enough to penetrate or pursue a matter. We must look at the upside and downside, then prioritize, focus and ignore. For our leadership to be impactful, we must know what to respond to and when.

Insight 13: Being Present With Your Ears Can Be More Valuable Than Being Present With Your Voice

There is much more to be gained by suppressing the desire to talk rather than dominating a conversation. Plato once said that: *"Wise men speak because they have something to say; fools because they have to say something."* We often miss opportunities, make mistakes and lose focus because we do not listen enough. It is always sad to watch people at the decision-making table trying to out-talk each other. On any given matter, most leaders have something to say. The ideas are never often complimentary but competing with people trying to pit their thought above another and refusing to listen to understand the value in that which others are saying. In situations like these, the problem may not necessarily be solved, but gets more complicated. No one likes a leader who does not listen. Assuming a listening stance reconfigures the leadership process. The listening leader creates a sense of psychological safety where individuals feel free to express uncertainty, confusion, and to communicate without fear.

> **"Wise men speak because they have something to say; fools because they have to say something."**

I was privileged to experience a leader who listened so much that all his meetings ran late. For him, it was more important to hear the perspective of all around the table than it was to keep time. Though he was knowledgeable and well skilled in many of the areas of concern, he would sit back in his chair with his hands in his lap and listen with a look of intrigue and amazement at the issues. He understood the principle that it was only through the experience of being heard that members' true authentic voices can find full expression. Whitney and Trosten-Bloom (2010) in their book, "Appreciative Leadership" stated that when individuals *"experience their ideas being listened to and validated, even if not acted on, they begin to share. When they see the leadership's commitment to open, honest communication, they follow."* Indeed, listening is a critical skill in leadership that can be learned and is an essential characteristic for an effective leader.

In completing my dissertation on leadership and leadership development at the University of Saskatchewan, Canada, my research concluded that listening is not only a skill but also a process. This conclusion was derived from a qualitative focus group and individual interviews from four participants from four different cultures. These were University Student Leaders who grew up in Canada, Kenya, Iran and Saudi Arabia. The participants in the research alluded to some critical stages in the listening process that if circumvented would prove to be ineffective.

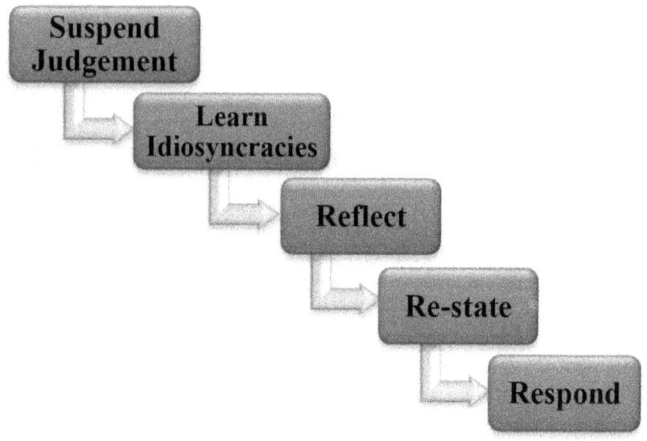

According to the participants, active listening necessitates a suspension of judgment and assumptions. When one suspends judgments then one can learn from others, and carefully sift through other points of view. After that first phase has taken place, the listener should reflect on what was heard. Reflection signifies a careful monitoring of the listener's developing assumptions as well as constantly analyzing, reorganizing and reasoning with what was heard. After the process of reflection, the listener should rearticulate or re-state what was heard to the speaker in order to ensure that what the speaker said matched what the speaker intended. It is only after the completion of suspending judgment, learning idiosyncrasies, reflecting, and re-stating that the listener should respond. This concept of active listening takes practice, but once mastered can be done unconsciously. The participants' convictions on the importance of listening actively to stakeholders demonstrated their willingness to learn, desire to serve, and humility in their leadership aura. The student leaders placed much value on listening in their leadership journey. They admired the listening quality in leaders, and it was one which they eagerly sought to develop. Listening, then, in leadership is not merely a desirable characteristic but a necessary process for leaders to operate in a respectful environment and earn the trust of employees.

> **Listening, then, in leadership is not merely a desirable characteristic but a necessary process for leaders to operate in a respectful environment and earn the trust of employees.**

Listening to others is a form of empowerment. When we listen to our colleagues, we add value to their perspectives, and we communicate that we accord much to their skills, capabilities and competencies. Recognizing that others bring unique gifts to the table that you, as a leader, just do not have is critical to how you progress in the leadership journey. Others need to be given a voice and a space to show that they can. They need to be trusted to do the work and then recognized for having done it well. No vision can be accomplished without an inner circle; a team of people who are enabled, empowered and entrusted with tasks, strategies and initiatives.

If you are doing most of the talking at the leadership table, you simply will not hear the fresh ideas and insights articulated by another. Your continuous talking will prevent you from challenging assumptions that may lie beneath the surface of the conversation. Developing a listening posture will add value to you rather than take it away. It will help you to interrogate and challenge information that will lead you to make wise decisions. Indeed, it takes a strong sense of security and abundance mind-set to release people, to show them to the world and to stand back and make others hear what they have to say. However, never forget that when your team members are shining, they shine on you and, in turn, your organization is illuminated. The highest priority then must be to listen to the voices of your employees, students, and colleagues and you will develop others so the success of the organization can be sustained, even when you are not around.

Insight 14: Learn Through Opportunities

It is a common practice for job descriptions to ask for experience. Having gone through over three thousand job descriptions across seventy-five organizations and over twenty-five professional groups in the public sector, I have seen where from the entry level all the way to the executive level, whether in a technical role or otherwise, experience is required. The younger generation among us often ask the question, "How do I get experience, if I am not given an opportunity?" This is a most seriously valid question as we do not only tend to forget that one must be given an opportunity to earn experience but, more importantly, experience can be gained in diverse, untraditional ways, often not discussed. Another point to note, and one that employers often do not interrogate, is that an employee's richness of capabilities does not necessarily lie in the years of their experiences but in the quality of their circumstances.

> An employee's richness of capabilities does not necessarily lie in the years of their experiences but in the quality of their circumstances.

It is time to change the way we look at opportunities. It does not have to be given to anyone. Good leaders and individuals with self-efficacy will not sit and wait to be handed ideas; they will put things in motion for great opportunities to emerge. Some will create it; others will seize it.

I remember vividly a young 25-year-old officer who joined the organization of which I was a part of two years ago. He came in with big ideas that were not necessarily aligned with his job description. He found creative ways to weave his ideas into his daily tasks and so re-imagined his work and defined his own space. He put his hand up to work across divisions and dabbled in areas he would consider outside of his comfort zone. He saw every area as an opportunity to learn, to stretch his competencies and to fortify himself in his workspace. Soon, he became a respected member of the team because of his adept knowledge of many areas of the organization and because of his multi-faceted mind. He did not only seize but created opportunities, making his job role one of the most envied across the organization.

The interesting thing is that, theoretically, the job description never changed. This shows that we do not need to limit ourselves to job descriptions. We do not need to function within a prescribed job function, or we will become

> **Leaders, and those who aspire to be, must consistently find ways to redefine their space and re-invent themselves.**

dysfunctional. Leaders, and those who aspire to be, must consistently find ways to redefine their space and re-invent themselves. Let us never assume that we know enough but rather consistently find ways to educate others and boost our productivity.

Insight 15: Learn To Give And Receive Feedback

Giving Feedback

Feedback is critical to building and sustaining good leadership. Good feedback is non-evaluative, non-judgemental, detailed and descriptive. Leaders ought to give feedback that is clear enough to stretch the mind of the recipient to do better. Feedback is not silence; it should be spoken or written. I have never forgotten a manager who once told me, when I asked him for feedback on my work, that, "no feedback is feedback." I was not only crushed but also disappointed in him as a leader.

> **Leaders ought to give feedback that is clear enough to stretch the mind of the recipient to do better.**

How can no feedback be feedback? The expectation, in this regard, is that employees should be able to read the minds of employers, make assumptions about their silence, and, therefore, reconfigure their work processes accordingly. Such an approach is inhumane, unreasonable, deeply draconian, and antagonistic. Silence from one's employer on his or her performance will only contribute to the development of a low trust environment. Feedback should be given, as it is a learning opportunity for others and ourselves.

When we give feedback, we learn about how the recipient viewed or interpreted the task given by listening to their explanation and responses. We learn about how we are perceived, whether we were unreasonable, unchallenging or unclear. We get an opportunity to work on our leadership behaviours that may be illuminated during the feedback process.

A rather instructive part of my journey that has changed the way I lead was a feedback I gave to one of my staff members on her performance in a stretch project she was asked to lead. In the feedback session, I expressed that I was not very pleased with her deliverable and expected much more from her. She asked me to articulate the "much more" I expected. In responding to her, I found that I had all these ideas in my head about the project that I never communicated. I had a vision for the project that I never shared, yet I expected her to deliver on my private thoughts. Her questions challenged me and

> The aim of any leader should always be a win-win for all involved in the process.

through them, I learned that I was being unfair in my evaluation of her. I have since learned to be very clear in what I want from a colleague and to consistently check and engage in conversations about how ideas are emerging. Clarifying expectations on an ongoing basis would have impacted her growth as well as mine. Clarity is key: clarity of the desired objective and clarity of the given task. The aim of any leader should always be a win-win for all involved in the process. We should never expect our employees to just know things we never communicated. If I had been clearer in my expectations, my staff member would have most likely succeeded, and the organization would have benefitted. Giving feedback should be mutually shaping, and empowering. Anything less can result in a divided and weakened organization or relationship, wasted energy, expense and conflict.

Receiving Feedback

On the other hand, feedback should also be received with a good attitude, however negative or caustic the feedback may have been. Though uncomfortable, we must learn to gauge our performance through the eyes of others. Feedback is not always about earning approval or feeling good about ourselves, but also seeing our gaps and finding ways to transform our thinking and mindset. Criticisms should be embraced and reflected upon as there is usually, always an opportunity to learn, re-examine a process and re-imagine a procedure. It is true that the person giving the feedback may mean to hurt, humiliate or demotivate you, but those motives are really of no moment, if we receive the feedback gracefully and purpose to use them as a springboard to become stronger and more formidable. A perceived weakness can become a strength if we choose to learn from the feedback of others.

Insight 16: Learning By Following Others

Everyone wants to be a leader indeed. It seems to be the holy grail in churches, homes, schools and companies. A follower, not so much. Good leadership, however, requires that we pay a lot more attention to the skill of "followership." Let's think about it. Followers and leaders do not live in separate universes. In some cases, leaders do not have superior skills that followers lack. There is an inextricable link between leadership and followership. The latter must never be seen as inferior. However, followership is a critical leadership construct that is often omitted from the leadership discussion. It is a skill that when a follower masters it, he or she is fit for leadership. Good leaders were often good followers. Through followership, we learn to

> **There is an inextricable link between leadership and followership.**

be accountable, to listen, develop emotional intelligence, value diversity, and see others as equals. A crucial variable in what makes organizations great is its followers; their high performing teams who tackle their tasks with tenacity and the highest degree of engagement.

Good leaders also follow their subordinates and follow them well. I may not be the very best person to lead a specific task or project. I, therefore, must learn to select an employee and follow that employee with the highest degree of respect. We must follow others regardless of hierarchy, if the individual we are following has demonstrated the capabilities in the area assigned. People do not need to be of a certain age or possess any great qualification or experience to lead well. In fact, age, experience and levels of qualification must never be assumed to be equated with effective leadership. Though these may be variables, we have seen from our discussion that effective leadership requires much more than age, qualification and experience.

> **In fact, age, experience and levels of qualification must never be assumed to be equated with effective leadership.**

Importantly, one does not have to be in a defined leadership role to be a leader of a team. Positions of hierarchy are secondary and often peripheral in the matter of leadership impact. People will follow you based on your influence, attitudes and values. Therefore, every single member of the organization is positioned to lead and to do so effectively. Regardless of where one falls on the organizational chart, the focus should be on the individual's output and the attitude or behaviours that accompany his or her deliverables.

In fact, the research on leadership continues to suggest that the concept of leader-follower dichotomy as a superior-inferior relationship process is fast eroding. Leadership models in the post-industrial era resemble a "web of inclusion;" depicting an architectural form more circular than hierarchical (Bolman & Deal; 2008; Helgesen, 1995). This definitive shift is presented in the diagram below:

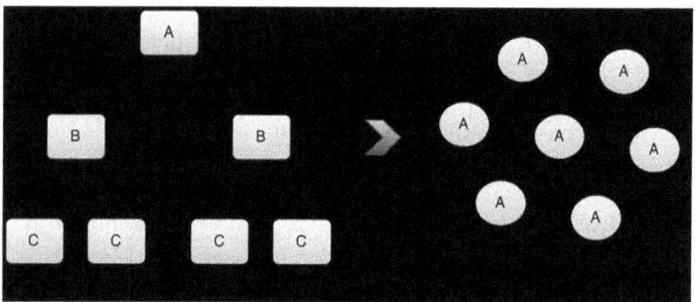

A representation of the paradigm shift of leadership: from industrial to post-industrial. Inspired by Berg (2003) and Helgensen (1995).

The post-industrial paradigm is focussed largely on the collaborative effort of the leaders and the followers in a mutually influential relationship "aimed at change for the common good" (Komives & Dugan, 2011, p. 40). Hirschhorn (1990) outlined that the need for leaders and their subordinates to recognize their dependence on each other is perhaps the most poignant demand in the post-industrial milieu. The leader, which is "A", no longer charts the organization with subordinates "B" and "C" lined up to do the bidding, rather everyone takes a leadership role; exercising community, collegiality, and shared decision-making.

In Helgensen's (1995) account of organizations as a web of inclusion, organizations are led from the center, and non-positional forms of power are honoured. The relationships among colleagues are inclusive and leaders can draw from a wide array of talents. In order to foster honest communication, transparency, and inclusivity, operating like a web is more efficient than the top-down structure. In the top-down structure, communication is unidirectional. The leader, "A", comes up with the ideas and the subordinates, "B" and "C", are expected to execute them. There is a clear division and hierarchy of influence. In the web-

> **Learning to follow and following others can be processes that are reflective, transforming and reforming.**

like structure, there is a flow of creativity. Ideas can come from anywhere in the organization and people are in touch directly with the leader. Each individual is seen as leader and there is a firm sense of participation in the leadership process (Helgensen, 1995). Learning to follow and following others can be processes that are reflective, transforming and reforming. This skill, often not embraced, is necessary for creating a world that is collaborative and engaging, rather than leader-centric and authority-oriented.

Reflecting On The *Learning* Dimension

The dimension of *Learning* teaches you how to overcome your limitations and grow from your setbacks and bad experiences. It challenges us to go forward and not lose focus based on our mistakes and failures. Learning is continuous. Regardless of our age, expertise, experiences and connections, we are at best ill-equipped to deal with the diverse personalities we meet on this journey. When we adopt a posture of learning, it changes the way we perceive things and influences how we treat and lead others. To be learning always means to be accepting that you are never at the place you need to be. It means you understand that there is much that you are unaware of, so you are seeking to remove the dissonance that exists between who you are and who you can become. It is the transitional phase that never ends but keeps looping repeatedly as you find out who you are, while executing your tasks and relating to others. It is at the learning phase that we develop the skills and competencies to do great things, to conceptualize and to implement. Through the pain and neglect, we develop confidence. Through the mistakes, we develop courage and tolerance and expand

> **Through the mistakes, we develop courage and tolerance and expand our capabilities.**

our capabilities. Through following others, we develop respect and trust and through ignoring, we develop even more self-awareness and self-control.

How much are you learning and willing to learn? As you reflect on the positives and painful experiences that have taught you powerful lessons, use the following guidelines to help you plan your growth.

a) Write down all the young leaders you know and challenge yourself to mentor and support as many of them as possible.

b) Think about a leader or person you may have rejected or demotivated. What exactly did you do or say to him or her? What steps will you take to ensure that you do not repeat the behaviour?

c) Reflect on the comments people make that trigger your emotions. Write down how they made you feel. Have you ever made those comments to others? Challenge yourself to **not** repeat the behaviour.

d) Go back to Insight 13 and examine the stages in the listening process. Try to practice at least two of the steps every time you listen until you have mastered them all.

e) Ask your colleagues, family or friends to give you feedback on any feedback you give to them. Listen carefully to their comments. Work through whether they were non-judgemental, detailed and descriptive.

DIMENSION 3

LEADERSHIP AS DOING

Make no little plans.
~ Daniel Burnham

Daniel Burnham, American Architect and Urban Planner, articulated a most stirring message more than a century ago. He said:

Make no little plans. They have no magic to stir men's blood and probably themselves will not be realized. Make big plans; aim high in hope and work, remembering that a noble, logical diagram once recorded will never die, but long after we are gone will be a living thing, asserting itself with ever-growing insistency. Remember that our sons and grandsons are going to do things that would stagger us. Let your watchword be order and your beacon beauty. Think big.

Leaders are the answers to a world fraught with problems. Leaders fix and make changes. We do not conserve and criticize. There is no movement, no momentum, no magic created by those who

> **Leaders are the answers to a world fraught with problems.**

sit and do nothing. Indeed, it is easier to criticize than to conceptualize, but we must remember that those who criticize will get attention but those who solve problems will be rewarded. What then is required in a world that seems to have a problem for every solution? What then is required for making a fledgling organization great? What then is required for sustaining systems that have proven worthy and generating ideas that can positively impact generations? The simple answer is this – leaders need to do, to act, to move things into motion. Leaders need to be able to move their organization to the place it needs to go. Have you ever met or worked with a leader who neither acts nor inspires others to act? The plans they make do not challenge the minds of others. They offer nothing challenging or risky to tackle. The qualities embedded

> **Indeed, it is easier to criticize than to conceptualize.**

in "Being" and 'Learning" are non-negotiable but not sufficient. However well we treat people, however much we listen and however much we learn, our leadership will still lack impact if we do not get things done. The kind of leadership that creates an atmosphere where people feel they belong and where they feel that their differences are valued is important. Unfortunately, these qualities are soon forgotten if leaders do not get results. The truth is, people want to see things happening; whether it is physical changes in the organization, which may include the construction of a new building and a redesigned entrance or enhancement of the spaces through painting or accessorizing. People want to see improvement in job processes, new ways of doing things, ease in customer service, and higher levels of productivity. At any level of the organization you are, people are interested in what you "do." This action-oriented approach is the sine qua non of leadership. Leaders need to show that they can strategize and successfully get the job done. Warren Bennis indicated that *"as leaders we can provide meaning, build trust and foster hope, but all that counts for little unless an organization produces results."* Leadership must be present, and leaders must show thrice as much dedication as their followers to succeed.

Effective leaders lead from a platform of performance and not potential or talks of accomplishments. Being able to do and get results will eventually silence critics and earn you the respect you need, build your reputation, and increase your confidence to get the organization to the next level. People want to see victories as victories indicate movement. As leaders, we must show that something is happening and to do so we must develop a proactive leadership spirit.

> **Effective leaders lead from a platform of performance and not potential or talks of accomplishments.**

Leadership is much more by example than precept. If gold rusts, what shall iron do? Collin Powell once said, *"You can issue all the memos and give all the motivational speeches you want, but if the rest of the people in the organization don't see you putting forth your very best effort every single day, they won't either."*

Insight 17: "Doing" Through Presence

The absentee leader is often spoken of because he or she is not around to hear what is being said in the cubicles, staffroom and offices. The leader who is present but absent in terms of impact is too detached to be hearing or observing what others think and feel. When one takes on the role of leadership, one must not only show up at work but be present and flat-footed, both hands on deck, mind engaged, and body and thoughts immersed in the tasks to accomplish. Anything less is unacceptable. We are given a job to do, to which we must be accountable and, whether we believe it or not, we will be judged for our stewardship. Results are achieved by taking action and moving with a sense of urgency.

I experienced an administrator in my second job as a teacher at a high school who operated from a premise that with urgency, things must be done. Her urgent approach to dealing with matters did not compromise due processes that should be followed or engaging stakeholders; rather those formed part of the urgency. She would swiftly move to activate all the processes needed to respond to a challenge. This sense of urgency and movement provided a kind of psychological safety among team members that they were part of an organization that was achieving tangible outcomes. Meetings would be followed by action points and development of work plans which would be carefully monitored to get the results envisioned. The goal was not to speak of things or to have things hanging as "in process" or "in progress", rather to get them done. Almost done or halfway there is not work done. Leaders need to see things through to the very end and to do this requires that they operate within structures.

Insight 18: "Doing" Through Structures

The term structure as a verb means to arrange, organise and design. As a noun, it refers to form, shape and composition. When we structure something, we organise or design it into a particular composition or shape. Operating with, or in structures, therefore, means to be engaged in processes with clear beginning and end processes, much like a blueprint of an architectural design or the recipe for making a meal or a checklist for a project. Without structure, creative ideas may never be implemented, and good initiatives may not be sustained. Operating in structure can create a major competitive advantage and generate a conviction that there will be a completion of the journey. People may often speak against structures on the basis that they may be rigid and limiting. However, at the other end we are faced with reactive approaches to situations because we did not plan properly. We must question whether we shy away from structures because our attention span may be such that we cannot take the time to conscientiously plan and implement. Are we more amenable to getting quick fixes that later prove problematic as a critical step

> **Operating in structure can create a major competitive advantage and generate a conviction that there will be a completion of the journey.**

or process was overlooked? Failing to operate in a structure may cause us to oversimplify complex issues and employ solutions only to the behaviours and events associated with problems, rather than focussing on the systems that may have caused the problems in the first place. In other words, without structures, we may end up addressing the symptom and not the disease.

Insight 19 - "Doing" Through Visioning

If you want to know if someone is truly connected to the work they are doing, ask them at any odd time of the day to articulate the vision of their organization. To get results, we must first know the results we want. I am not referring to only the immediate results of a project but its long-term impact. Leaders should be able to articulate how a work process or initiative can spur the organization to growth, and what benefits can be derived from it. He or she must be able to see the difference between the ideas that can build the organization as opposed to those that can maintain and change it. The leader's action must be one that is targeted as there is a driving force, a motivation behind every move.

My favourite novel from Shakespeare is "Hamlet" and I have read them all. I continue to be particularly intrigued by Polonius' statement in Hamlet, Act I, Scene 2, *"though this be madness, yet there is method in it."* The statement suggests that there is a purpose that is driving his actions, however much he may seem crazy. Leading with a vision does not only suggest that one is doing something but also that one is assured of results. It also compels one to set priorities and to redirect processes when things are moving out of alignment with the vision. Doing with the vision in mind helps leaders to focus on the "business of the business", that is, what are the crucial things that must be done now to achieve the desired target? What partnership should we accept or reject? What values should we promote? What skillsets need to be broadened? Who do we need to engage and when? Vison gets our organizations focussed and to ponder about the things that really matter. Vision gets leaders to see the big picture in the tiny details. The tiny details do not distract but serve as reinforcement to achieving the big picture. Inability to see the big picture will cause us to represent every tiny detail as a conclusion. On the other hand, a lack of vision gives a rather myopic view of how things are. The story of the six blind men and the elephant illustrates the dangers involved in not being able to see the big picture:

> **Inability to see the big picture will cause us to represent every tiny detail as a conclusion.**

It was six men of Indostan,
To learning much inclined,
Who went to see the Elephant
(Though all of them were blind),
That each by observation
Might satisfy his mind.

The First approach'd the Elephant,
And happening to fall
Against his broad and sturdy side,
At once began to bawl:
"God bless me! But the Elephant
Is very like a wall!"

The Second, feeling of the tusk,
Cried, —, "Ho! What have we here
So very round and smooth and sharp?
To me 'tis mighty clear,
This wonder of an Elephant
Is very like a spear!"

The Third approach'd the animal,
And happening to take
The squirming trunk within his hands,
Thus boldly up and spake:

"I see," —quoth he— "the Elephant
Is very like a snake!"

The Fourth reached out an eager hand,
And felt about the knee:
"What most this wondrous beast is like
Is mighty plain," —quoth he,—
"'Tis clear enough the Elephant
Is very like a tree!"

The Fifth, who chanced to touch the ear,
Said— "E'en the blindest man
Can tell what this resembles most;
Deny the fact who can,
This marvel of an Elephant
Is very like a fan!"

The Sixth no sooner had begun
About the beast to grope,
Then, seizing on the swinging tail
That fell within his scope,
"I see," —quoth he,— "the Elephant
Is very like a rope!"

And so these men of Indostan
Disputed loud and long,
Each in his own opinion

Exceeding stiff and strong,
Though each was partly in the right,
And all were in the wrong!

MORAL:

So, oft in theological wars
The disputants, I ween,
Rail on in utter ignorance
Of what each other mean;
And prate about an Elephant
Not one of them has seen!

The ability to see beyond the surface and to illuminate the pieces, not as pieces but as functions of part of a whole is the responsibility of the leader. More than anyone else, the designated head of the organization is the chief cheerleader, chief fun officer, and chief motivator. The leader moves the people beyond short-term thinking to infinite possibilities. The leader helps you to realize that you are not merely performing routine tasks, but you are building an organization. The leader is the driving force behind the effort of the team and when the leader wanes, two things can happen:

> **The leader moves the people beyond short-term thinking to infinite possibilities.**

1. Another leader emerges or
2. The organization crumbles.

Insight 20: "Doing" Through Core Values

A story was told of a school that was burning down and there were fire extinguishers in the school's staffroom. All the teachers were sitting debating on what the principal would do if he were present. While the school burned and the fire extinguishers stood firmly on the staffroom wall, the teachers concluded that they do not know what to do, as they could not predict what action the principal would take and what action he would accept. Without a doubt, the school burned to the ground. Everything was destroyed. This story illustrates that the leader did not operate with any set value or principle. His behaviours were unpredictable because he did not lead from a platform of values. His actions, therefore, proved destructive to his organization. When we do leadership without values, we lead with inconsistency. Values are necessary for consistency in action and predictability of leadership behaviours. Values are the deeply ingrained principles that guide our actions and behaviours; they serve as our moral compass. They drive the

> Values are necessary for consistency in action and predictability of leadership behaviours.

way we interact, influence and work with others to achieve goals and the strategic objectives of our organizations. They influence how we lead, and they offer onlookers a good perspective of who we are. Knowing what these are and changing or honouring them will not only be critical to our leadership success, but also to our personal and spiritual achievements. Conversely, a failure to understand or adhere to our values can lead to weakened relationships, low self esteem, lack of self-confidence and poor performance which will impact negatively on the quality of the service we provide to our colleagues, thereby adversely affecting our leadership environment. Often, values are shown through slogans or framed words hanging from a wall. This, by itself, cannot create impact; words on a page cannot get results. Leaders are required to live the values they espouse for performance to happen. If punctuality is a core value, then the leaders should endeavour to turn up early to meetings. If caring is a core value, then the leaders should demonstrate empathy and compassion throughout his or her practices. If integrity is a core value, then the leaders should emphasize integrity in speech and treatment towards others. Values such as fairness, justice, equity and respect for human dignity are often not seen as a springboard for action, but they are. If we lack these, what movements are we prepared to make to create 'better' for others and ourselves. Leaders must remain conscious that their behaviour may form the character of the next generation who will assume the role of leadership. Doing otherwise might result in the complete breakdown of a society's moral structure. The core values we embrace should not only be evident in our actions but should also propel us to action.

> **The core values we embrace should not only be evident in our actions but should also propel us to action.**

I honour greatly the values of fairness, justice, equity and respect for human dignity. These values have defined how I operate at home, work and in every other sphere. Injustice moves my heart to want to make a change. I embarked on studying law for the singular reason that I abhor injustice. Leaders need to have a clear conviction about what they will accept and what they will reject. Having values makes this very clear. It positions one to distinguish between wisdom and foolishness, right and wrong. It prepares one to be unfettered by opposition and to obey the unenforceable. Indeed, leaders can accomplish much through speaking of and living by values. We do have too many leaders who operate on the Dr. Jekyll and Mr. Hyde's approach, embracing manipulation and duplicity. These behaviours reflect instability and will generate:

- Hesitation where there should be action.
- Weakness where there should be strength.
- Doubt where there should be certainty.
- Fear where there should be courage.
- Silence where one should be speaking boldly.

Values are the anchors and without them, we get lost in a world trying to please everyone and trying to respond to every criticism. When you lead from a platform of values, though you may not be loved, you will be respected. I have come to learn, just by experience, that at the end of the day, everybody wants good leadership. No matter how people complain and sabotage each other in the workplace, church or school, ***we all desire a leader who leads***. We wait for our leaders' responses to situations. We analyse their treatment of others and, most of all, we measure their actions against the universal codes of right and wrong, fairness and unfairness, good and bad. Whatever those codes are, inexplicable or otherwise, we hold our leaders to them. We forget their charisma. We argue away their knowledge. We eventually scoff at their wit and rhetoric and fall asleep in their

> **When you lead from a platform of values, though you may not be loved, you will be respected.**

sermons. The goal, therefore, must always be as King David says in II Samuel 23 vs 3 and 4:

> *The God of Israel said, the Rock of Israel spake to me, He that ruleth over men must be just, ruling in the fear of God. And he shall be as the light of the morning, when the sun riseth, even a morning without clouds; as the tender grass springing out of the earth by clear shining after rain.*

When we take on leadership roles, however challenging, daunting or rewarding, one thing is expected of us, which is foundational and non-negotiable. That expectation is fairness; not an appearance of fairness, but fairness. Without fairness:

Strategy is short-lived
Decisions are questionable
Communication is filtered
Authority is undermined
Promises are scoffed at
Trust is eroded
Productivity is diminished.

I AM COMMITTED TO *DOING*

I will rewind time by more than a decade to tell my story of being committed to "doing." It started with a desire to understand leadership and leadership development from a more theoretical and philosophical level to effectively apply it to practice. I had already completed my Masters' of Philosophy in Foreign Language Education and having focussed on leadership in three struggling secondary high schools, I was restless to do something about the entire leadership landscape of schools. My entire being said to me that there is a problem, which I will not join in lamenting but will be a part of the solution. I, therefore, applied to the University of Saskatchewan in Canada, College of Education, to pursue my Doctor of Philosophy. I had no money. I had no family in that part of the world. I had no network of support. I had no sponsors. I had no help. However, I had a conviction and a husband who also believed.

We needed to have a minimum of sixteen thousand Canadian dollars to qualify for the student visa. Taking my three-year-old daughter with me to Canada was a non-negotiable that we had established from the beginning. My husband was in the Army and his job would require him spontaneously to be out in any given emergency. There was no way I was going to ask my mother to raise another child, after she gracefully raised five of her own and, for the most part, as a single mother. My daughter was coming with me. I was adamant.

We decided to strategize how we would ethically earn this money in order to go to the embassy. We had about seven months to make it happen. The first thing we decided to do was sell the twelve-year-old car I drove to work. Having sold the car, we had about a quarter of the money we needed. My husband then sold his sixteen-year-old car. We saved all the money from salary that we could. We minimised on grocery and were very cautious with the use of electricity and water at home. We knew we had to make this money to achieve the dream that God put into my heart. I was a teacher of Spanish and I also taught extra classes for students who were enrolled to sit the Caribbean Secondary Schools Examinations. For every money earned, I would take a little trip to the Western Union that was located just behind my workplace and buy Canadian dollars. I would buy five dollars, fifteen dollars, twenty-five dollars. I would then go to the bank and deposit it in the account we had opened for that purpose.

For a sustained seven months, we were focussed, and we were able to save ten thousand Canadian dollars. We were short by six thousand dollars and we could not conceive another way to make it. I said to my husband, "We have no choice. We have to go to the embassy." Being the logical and pragmatic thinker, he said, "We are below what we need. It is a risk." I said, "But we either go or abandon this venture." We decided to take the risk and go to the embassy with the limited money that we had.

On the given date, we went and submitted the documents. After about three weeks, on a Tuesday, about midday in July, I got a phone call. When I answered the phone, I was greeted with an accent and I knew immediately it was a representative from the embassy. After she greeted me, she said, "You have applied for a student visa for yourself, and visas for your husband and daughter to accompany you to Canada."

"Yes," I affirmed.

"Will your daughter and husband be staying with you for the period of study?" she asked.

I replied, "Well my husband will only be with us to settle us in, but my daughter will be with me for the entire period."

She then remarked, "But you do not have enough money to sustain a three-year old. It will cost you at least six hundred dollars per month for day care. The money you have now cannot sustain that."

Without shrieking, I said, "Thanks so much, but if my daughter cannot stay with me, I am not going."

There was a pause and then she said, "You can collect the passports at the DHL office in Kingston in about two weeks."

I concluded that I would be picking up passports with no visas and my dream of getting the exposure I needed to this critical concept was lost. For the next week, I started to re-adjust my thoughts. I stopped talking about travelling to Canada to pursue my studies and I forced myself to stop thinking about it too. I did not want to confront the reality of a dream deferred. It was a torment. In about twelve days, after the phone call, I got another call. That call was the one that communicated the date and time to pick up the passports.

I remember calling my husband and he arranged for transportation to take us to the DHL office. Upon arrival, I tried to settle in my heart that it was not my time and maybe it was just not for me to begin with. I walked into the office and presented my identification. A closed package was given to me that contained the documents. We did open the passports in the office because we expected the outcome to be passports without visas. When we went back to the car, I opened the package and skimmed through my passport as a matter of reflex. To my amazement, there was a student visa, nicely posted on the page.

My husband pulled over the car and said, "Wait, T, they gave you the visa? Look and see if they gave Chrysali."

I said, "Let me check yours first because if they gave it to you, then they must have also given it to her." We checked his and it was there. He got it too. We beamed with excitement. We then checked our daughter's passport and, without fail, there it was. I remember saying aloud, "This has to be the Christ."

I got an opportunity that only Christ could give. Monetarily, we were not qualified. We, however, had certain convictions and principles that God chose to honour. We chose to put in the work to get there by saving what we could, and we chose not to leave our child behind. Having received the visas, I decided I was going to give this opportunity one hundred percent of myself and I would return to my country and give a hundred percent. I was committed to "doing" my best.

By the end of my first year, I got a scholarship for twenty thousand Canadian dollars and an opportunity to teach at the University level. I completed my studies in record time in spite of all the challenges I faced every day. I had challenges with racism. I was black in a very white part of the world. I had my struggles. I walked my daughter to and from school, even in the snow that lasted almost half a year. Still, I got up every day. I showed up everyday and rejected doing or submitting mediocre work.

I budgeted carefully and was able to save money from my scholarship fund. When I completed, I relentlessly pursued and secured a job in my home country. I returned home with an inner drive that moved me into action every day.

I continued my journey of leadership knowing I had to think at a higher level, strategize, listen more than speak, control my emotions and support those set above me. I needed to be a good steward with the talents, gifts, tasks and people God had entrusted to me. I quickly came to understand that going to Canada was never about achieving the terminal degree; it was about what it took to achieve it. It was never about studying in a foreign country; it was about the lessons you learn by being there. It was not about fulfilling my dreams; it was about being a good steward and being obedient to God's calling. My friend, it is never about the destination; it is about what you do on the journey.

When we are given something to do, we must maximize all the gifts we have been given to do it. We must seek out other talents, bring on board others who have the skills we lack, and purpose to deliver at the highest level. We will give an account for what we did with what we had.

In work, in family, in friendship, the "doing" defines us. What we do separates us from everyone else, making us unique, without rival, incomparable to the crowd. We build our teams by what we say, think, learn, experience and, ultimately, by what we do.

If we are serious about creating capabilities and bringing out the best in those purposefully placed in our spaces, we must ensure that there is synergy between our words and our actions.

ABOUT THE AUTHOR

Taneisha Ingleton, PhD** has a performance driven, agile and innovative mind. She believes in the infinite capacity of each individual to bring autonomy, mastery and purpose to their life and work. She is a Leadership Development Programme Designer, Educational Leadership Researcher and Facilitator, Capability Development Specialist, Consultant and Designer of Competency Frameworks. She earned her PhD at the University of Saskatchewan, Canada. Her scholarly writing, experiences and dissertation research have focused significantly on leadership development. Prior to her Master of Philosophy Degree, she had completed her Undergraduate Degree and Post Graduate Diploma from the University of the West Indies [UWI], Jamaica with First Class Honours and distinction respectively. Dr. Ingleton has over seventeen years combined teaching, research and management experience at the high school level, Undergraduate, Masters and PhD levels in Jamaica and Canada. Her areas of research and teaching include Educational Leadership, Educational Policy and Planning, Instructional Leadership, School Improvement, Strategic Planning, Editorial Writing, Spanish Language, Literature and Culture. She has published papers on the Principalship, Transformational Leadership, and School Effectiveness. Dr. Ingleton was critical to the development of the Whole of Government Competency Framework and Professional Pathways for the Public Service in Jamaica. She is a certified Performance Coach, a motivational and sought-after keynote speaker on matters relating to leadership development, creating a culture of continuous improvement, authenticity and personal and professional advancement. Dr. Taneisha Ingleton resides in Jamaica with her husband, Carmichael, and their daughter, Chrysali.

END NOTES

Insight 1

1. Decharms, R., Carpenter, V., & Kuperman, A. (1965). The "origin-pawn" variable in person perception. *Sociometry*, 28(3), 241-258.

Insight 2

1. Deitch, J. (2018). Elevate: An essential guide to life. Texas, Greenleaf Book Group Press.

Insight 6

1. Bolman, L., & Deal, T. (2008). Reframing organizations: Artistry, choice and leadership (3rd ed). San Francisco: Jossey-Bass.

Insight 7

1. Ingleton, T. (2014). Appreciative voices on leadership and leadership development. Saskatoon, The University of Saskatchewan

Insight 8

1. Henderlong, J., & Lepper, M. R. (2002). The effects of praise on children's intrinsic motivation: A review and synthesis. *Psychological Bulletin,* 128(5), 774-795.

2. Kohn, Alfie (1986). No Contest: The case against competition. New York: Houghton Mifflin Company.

Insight 13

1. Whitney, D., Trosten-Bloom, A, & Rader, K. (2010). Appreciative leadership: Focus on what works to drive winning performance and build a thriving organization. New York: McGraw Hill.

Insight 15

1. Helgesen, S. (1995). The web of inclusion: A new architecture for building great organizations. New York: Currency/Doubleday.

2. Komives, S.R. & Dugan, J.P. (2011). Leadership theories. In In S.R. Komives., J.P. Dugan, J.E. Owen, C. Slack, W. Wagner, & Associates (Eds.), *The handbook for student leadership development* (2nd ed. pp. 35-57). San Francisco: Jossey-Bass.

3. Hirschhorn, L. (1990). Leaders and followers in a post-industrial age. *Journal of Applied Behavioral Science,* 26, 529-542. doi: 10.1177/0021886390264008

www.ingramcontent.com/pod-product-compliance
Lightning Source LLC
Chambersburg PA
CBHW050647160426
43194CB00010B/1848